A Rockpool book
PO Box 252
Summer Hill
NSW 2130
Australia

rockpoolpublishing.com
Follow us! f ⃝ rockpoolpublishing
Tag your images with #rockpoolpublishing

Northern hemisphere edition
ISBN: 9781922579287

Published in 2023 by Rockpool Publishing
Copyright text © Flavia Kate Peters and Barbara Meiklejohn-Free 2023
Images from Shutterstock

Design by Daniel Poole, Rockpool Publishing
Edited by Lisa Macken

Printed and bound in China
10 9 8 7 6 5 4 3 2 1

RECLAIMING THE MAGICK OF THE OLD WAYS

2024 WITCH'S DIARY

NORTHERN HEMISPHERE

FLAVIA KATE PETERS · BARBARA MEIKLEJOHN-FREE

ROCKPOOL

PIONEERS OF THE CRAFT

The *2024 Witch's Diary* honours all those who have given their lives to the craft. They are the founders, wisdom keepers, elders and leaders who have gone before us, ensuring that we today hold the sacred knowledge of the ancients despite the gruesome punishments many faced and still face in mainstream society and particular cultures for their beliefs.

Let us remember those seen and unseen, known and unknown, and give our undying gratitude to all those who have shone the light of magick through the darkness.

We witches stand now side by side, strong in our beliefs while the ancestors walk beside us, and we are proud to call ourselves witches of the craft.

So mote it be.

HAIL AND WELCOME!

Does your heart feel the pull of nature? Do you hear the whispers of the ancestors on the breeze? Do you bask in the power of the sun and harness the magick of the moon? Do you welcome the seasons and yearn for a deep connection with the earth? Witches have been around since the beginning of time, harnessing magick and connecting with higher powers. They were the wise ones of the village, who used their knowledge of nature to heal the sick and restore balance to the world.

The *2024 Witch's Diary*, a magickal tool from which you can draw ancient wisdom, enables you to thrive in balance and harmony with a sprinkle of very real magick. This practical guide will show you how to harness the magick of nature, claim your personal power through the discovery of ancient wisdom and embrace the divine feminine. As you journey through the year you'll learn how to work with the forces of nature through spell work, incantations, rituals, sigils, age-old recipes and charms that use herbs, candles and crystals.

Witches are everywhere. A witch embraces each season and rejoices at every new bud during the first stirrings of spring, the harvest abundance that summer supplies and the falling leaves of autumn, and revels in the deep, dark mystery that accompanies the winter months.

A witch's heart sings at the mere notion of magick, has an affinity with the ways of natural healing and believes in another world of mystical beings. The natural witch is able to connect with this 'other' world, perceiving and working in conjunction with the ancestors, whose wisdom and guidance can be drawn from. This is the way of the witch. A witch is a healer who embraces the workings of nature and takes a responsible attitude in guardianship for our beloved planet and those who reside on it.

Now more than ever you are being urged to awaken the witch within and integrate with the magick and mystery of yesteryear. As you walk along the ancient path of the witch and as an advocate of the old ways, you'll find freedom to express who you truly are and reclaim your personal power.

The *2024 Witch's Diary* is ideal for any nature lover who wishes to bring the magick of the old ways into their everyday lives. Each month you'll discover how to work with specific moon phases and weekdays in order to harness your personal power and enhance your magickal abilities.

This diary is perfect for both seasoned witches or for those who are exploring the ancient path of the wise. Each page is a magickal avenue to draw upon venerable wisdom that is still relevant for the modern witch today.

You'll find each page assists you well
Through incantation, message, spell
Tools explained, history unearthed
Allowing magick to be birthed
The witch in you will be empowered
No more will others leave you soured
Look no further than inside
It's here the magick doth reside.

Blessed be,
Flavia and Barbara

MOON PHASES

The moon has always fascinated humankind, its luminosity hinting at our celestial origins, and it's no wonder the ancients worshipped it as the goddess herself. All things in life are interconnected, so the frequencies emanating from the moon can affect your feelings and emotions. When you become acquainted with the moon's phases you'll know when to cast certain spells and when to access its energies for its particular transformational powers.

~ Dark or old moon ~
This phase is a powerful time to remove and banish things, people or situations, a time to neutralise spells made against others. It's also a potent time for understanding your fears and anger and bringing about justice.

*Time of transition from the
dark moon to a new moon.*

~ Waxing crescent moon ~
This phase is for constructive magick to increase things, fresh beginnings and relationships and sowing seeds for new ventures. It's the best time to set your intentions for positive outcomes.

~ First quarter moon ~
This phase is the optimum time for drawing in things such as money, success, friends, lovers and work, and for attracting what you most desire into manifestation. It also indicates a period of acceleration and growth.

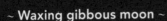

~ Waxing gibbous moon ~

This phase is about the renewal of strength and energy. It's a time to focus on willpower and seeing things through and surrender to the universe and trust. This is the most powerful moon phase for fruition and completion.

~ Full moon ~

During a full moon what no longer serves you will be released and you can harness extra power to overcome difficult challenges. This is a time of manifestation, when you can use rituals and spells for protection and divination and heal long-standing illness. A full moon is the most powerful one and its magick is potent.

~ Waning gibbous moon ~

This is a great time to expel all negative thoughts and influences. Waning moon energies rid and repel, so it's a time to decrease and bring things to an end and a time of facing your shadows.

~ Last quarter moon ~

This is a phase of transitions, and for removing obstacles and avoiding temptations.

~ Waning crescent moon ~

With this phase comes a transition between the death of the old and the birth of the new. It's a time of banishment and retreat.

Between a dark moon and a waxing crescent moon is a period of stillness called the new moon, which is the space between the past and new beginnings. This is a very powerful phase of transition.

LUNAR AND
SOLAR ECLIPSES

Eclipses are magickal astrological events that can fuel a witch's intentions, wishes and spells with cosmic energy to manifest new beginnings and empowering, positive change.

Solar eclipses occur during a new moon. When the sun, moon and earth are in alignment the moon casts a shadow across the earth that fully or partially blocks out the sun. For witches, a solar eclipse means harnessing the magick of new beginnings to truly transform.

Lunar eclipses occur only during a full moon. When the sun and earth are in close alignment with the moon it moves into the earth's shadow and becomes fully or partially obscured. For witches, a lunar eclipse means harnessing the magick of empowerment and manifestation.

2024

24–25 March: penumbral lunar eclipse

8 April: total solar eclipse

17–18 September: partial lunar eclipse

2 October: annular solar eclipse

17 October: almost total lunar eclipse

2025

13–14 March: total lunar eclipse

29 March: partial solar eclipse

7–8 September: total lunar eclipse

21 September: partial solar eclipse

FULL MOONS

A full moon usually happens once a month, and when there are two full moons in a month the second one is called a blue moon. During a full moon phase manifesting magick is at its optimum. Each full moon has a variety of names relating to the month and a unique mystical energy that can be harnessed to enhance your magickal workings.

JANUARY: olde, frost, birch, cold moon.
Letting go of the past and invoking the new.

FEBRUARY: ice, snow, rowan, quickening moon.
The journey of the soul inwards.

MARCH: moon of winds, storm, ash, worm, crow moon.
Coming from the darkness and growing into the light.

APRIL: growing, alder, seed moon.
Growth and the planting of new ideas.

MAY: hare, milk, bright, willow moon.
Attention to your needs and the needs of those you love.

JUNE: moon of horses, hawthorn, strawberry moon.
Balance and understanding.

JULY: hay, thunder, mead, oak moon.
Making plans for the future.

AUGUST: corn, holly, grain moon.
Removing excess baggage and being flexible.

SEPTEMBER: harvest, hazel, fruit, barley moon.
Completion and future prospects.

OCTOBER: blood, vine, hunter's moon.
Soul growth and deep inner wisdom.

NOVEMBER: snow, ivy, dark moon.
Truth and honesty while reassessing your life.

DECEMBER: wolf, elder, cold moon.
Healing old wounds and emotions.

THE WHEEL OF THE YEAR

Spiritual wisdom can be gained by recognising the traditions of old witchcraft and the connection to the seasons. As the witches of old worked with the elemental forces of nature they also honoured the aspects of the triple goddess in relation to the seasons and festivals celebrated through the wheel of the year.

In nature, the year is made up of four seasons. The sun marks any seasonal change, and these changes are honoured by celebrating four solar festivals. Fire festivals are marked by cross-quarter and equinox celebrations, so altogether eight festivals of the seasons become the wheel of the year. These festivals represent the state of nature at the time, the agricultural calendar and the physical and spiritual effects the time of year has on humankind.

From planting in spring to harvesting in autumn, the seasons are of great importance. Different celebrations mark times to count your blessings, for reaping and recognising all that you've sown and for giving thanks to nature spirits and the goddess in her triple aspect of maiden, mother and crone as she continues the circle that is called life on earth.

CROSS-QUARTER FESTIVALS AND EQUINOXES

IMBOLC, 1 February: this is a time of fresh growth, as new shoots appear from the ground, early shoots begin to show and we begin to witness the start of the renewal of life. The maiden: innocence, purity, seeding the dream and birthing the inner child.

OSTARA, 20 March: this is a time when balance hangs in the air, the length of day equals that of night and the birth of new life is celebrated. The maiden matures: from dark to light we explore signs of growth and discernment.

BELTANE, 1 May: this fire festival celebrates the full bloom of nature. The mother: fertile minds, bodies and souls, birthing your ideas and soul's knowing.

LITHA, 21 June: this festival celebrates the summer solstice, the longest day of the year. The mother glorified: a celebration of light and being in your full glory.

LUGHNASADH, 1 August: the time when the grain harvest is cut down and celebrated. The mother matures: gratitude for earthly, physical sustenance.

MABON, 21–24 September: during this time day and night are balanced and the fruit harvest is celebrated. The crone: the art of contemplation is explored and there is self-sufficiency of mind, body and spirit.

SAMHAIN, 31 October: a time to honour the souls of the dead, when the veil between the worlds is at its thinnest. The crone revered: respecting your ancestors and healing your hurts.

YULE, 20–23 December: the winter solstice is a celebration of the rebirth of the sun, for now that the longest night has arrived the days start to grow longer. The crone fades: the returning sun and an exploration of the purest energy that is the essence of your being.

PLANTING AND HARVESTING DAYS

Witches have always planted according to the moon cycles and in conjunction with the movement of the planets, because they understand that different plants grow better when they are planted during different phases of the moon. Each moon phase imparts an influence on the way vegetation grows through the rising and falling of the moisture in the ground and in the plants: how the plant stores water in the fruit/crop at different times of the moon cycle is critical. It's not just planting that is the most important time for the farmer: harvest time also has to be considered, as harvesting at the correct time ensures crops last much longer.

NEW MOON: an excellent time to sow leafy plants such as cabbages, broccoli, celery and cauliflowers and transplant leafy annuals.

WAXING MOON: sap flows and rises, so this is a good time for new growth. Sow or transplant flowering annuals, biennials and grains and plant fruits or flowers that are to be harvested.

FIRST QUARTER MOON: this is the time to plant tomatoes, beets, broccoli, beans and squash.

FULL MOON: during a full moon sow or plant root crops such as potatoes and asparagus and fruit perennials such as apples and rhubarb. This is the perfect time for separating plants and taking cuttings.

WANING MOON: sap is drawn down during a waning moon, so plant perennials and root crops. It's a good time to prune and harvest.

LAST QUARTER MOON: this is the time to weed, dig or plough and improve the soil with compost or manure.

PLANET RULERS AND SIGNS

Each zodiac sign is affiliated with a planet that is said to be its ruler. The ruling planet adds a dimension and influence to the sign it rules and influences how the sign is expressed, which gives insights into the personality traits intrinsic within the sign.

ARIES
Mars

LIBRA
Venus

TAURUS
Venus

SCORPIO
Mars

GEMINI
Mercury

SAGITTARIUS
Jupiter

CANCER
The moon

CAPRICORN
Saturn

LEO
The sun

AQUARIUS
Uranus

VIRGO
Mercury

PISCES
Neptune

THE GODDESS AND MOON PHASES

The goddess is worshipped in conjunction with the phases of the moon – waxing, full and waning – which represent the three phases of the goddess as maiden, mother and crone.

~ MAIDEN ~

ASPECTS: beauty, enchantment, inception, expansion, new beginnings, youth, excitement, virginity, innocence.

Season: spring.

Colour: white.

Moon phase: waxing.

Festivals: Imbolc, Ostara (spring equinox).

~ MOTHER ~

ASPECTS: ripeness, fertility, growth, fulfilment, stability, giving, nurturing, compassion.

Season: summer.

Colour: red.

Moon phase: full.

Festivals: Beltane, Litha (summer solstice), Mabon (autumn equinox).

~ CRONE ~

ASPECTS: wisdom, repose, magick, destruction, decay, death.

Season: winter.

Colour: black.

Moon phases: waning, dark, new.

Festivals: Samhain (Hallowe'en), Yule (winter solstice).

MAGICKAL WEEKDAYS

Witches adhere to specific magickal timings such as weekdays to enhance their magickal practice and so they can work with universal energies while they are at their most potent in relation to the chosen spell.

~ SUNDAY ~

The day of the god Apollo, ruled by the sun: this day is imbued with energy and divine guidance and is perfect for relaxing and unwinding and focusing on health and well-being to light up your inner sunshine.

~ MONDAY ~

The day of the goddess Diana, ruled by the moon: this is a day for discovering your true potential and intuition and looking deep within and honouring your emotions.

~ TUESDAY ~

The day of the god Týr, ruled by Mars: a day for projects, new jobs and decision-making and to take steps to fulfil your goals and desires.

~ WEDNESDAY ~

The day of the god Woden (Odin), ruled by Mercury: a day to express yourself and focus on life decisions and for communication and messages.

~ THURSDAY ~

The day of the god Thor, ruled by Jupiter: a day of gratitude and positivity and a time of expansion of your mind, body and spirit.

~ FRIDAY ~

The day of the goddess Frigg, ruled by Venus: a day of love and self-care and a time to create and connect with others.

~ SATURDAY ~

The day of the god Saturn: a great day to tackle big projects and be responsible and get organised both at home and at work. It's also a time to be grounded and balanced.

MAGICKAL MOON TIMES
TO CAST SPELLS

~ DARK MOON ~
from dawn until sunset.

~ WAXING CRESCENT MOON ~
from mid-morning until after sunset.

~ FIRST QUARTER MOON ~
from noon until midnight.

~ WAXING GIBBOUS MOON ~
from mid-afternoon until 3 am.

~ FULL MOON ~
from sunset until dawn.

~ WANING GIBBOUS MOON ~
from mid-evening until mid-morning.

~ LAST QUARTER MOON ~
from midnight until noon.

~ WANING CRESCENT MOON ~
from 3 am until mid-afternoon.

MAGICKAL MEANINGS OF COLOURS

Colour is a natural source of cosmic energy that a witch can draw upon. Every colour has its own unique vibration and resonance that can be harnessed for magickal spells and healing and used in the form of, for example, coloured candles, cloth or crystals.

~ BLACK ~

elimination, banishment, retribution, north, earth.

~ BLUE ~

peace, harmony, healing, curing fevers, reuniting friends, house blessings.

~ BROWN ~

grounding, stabilisation, intuition, balance, connection to Mother Earth.

~ GREEN ~

fertility, good fortune, generosity, wealth, success, renewal, marriage, healing.

~ GOLD ~

cosmic influences, solar deities, success, wealth, influence.

~ INDIGO ~

meditation, balancing karma, stopping gossip, astral projection.

~ MAGENTA ~

rapid change, spiritual healing, exorcism.

~ ORANGE ~

communication, telepathy, new job, adaptability, luck, control, attraction.

~ PINK ~

romance, affection, love, spiritual awakening, unity.

~ PURPLE ~

honour, respect, wisdom, divine knowing, trust, spiritual connection.

~ SILVER ~

moon magick, protection from entities, inner peace, serenity.

~ WHITE ~

purification, blessings, aspect of light, cosmos.

MAGICKAL DIRECTIONS AND ELEMENTS

Each direction is assigned to one of the four basic elements of earth, air, fire and water; without them, this planet would be lifeless. The four basic elements work in harmony with each other and with the fifth element of spirit, which runs through everything to create and sustain life. Each of the four basic elements is associated with a direction, season and moon phase when it comes to magickal workings, and we acknowledge above, below and within. Witches work naturally with the forces of nature and call upon the guardians of each direction when creating sacred space and before ritual and spell casting.

~ NORTH ~
the element of earth and the season of winter; *a time of the new moon and midnight.*

~ WEST ~
the element of water and the season of autumn; *a time of the waning moon and dusk.*

~ EAST ~
the element of air and the season of spring; *a time of the waxing moon and sunrise.*

~ SOUTH ~
the element of fire and the season of summer; *a time of the full moon and noon.*

~ ABOVE ~
mind connection with the universal great mystery.

~ BELOW ~
body connection with the earth.

~ WITHIN ~
spirit connection with your inner universe, the great void.

TREES OF POWER

Ancient and enduring and known as the standing ones, trees are wisdom keepers and mystical gateways to the otherworld. Trees have long been associated with witches, for they hold the magickal secrets of yesteryear and are extreme sources of power a witch can draw upon. The spirits of the trees are multidimensional and they each have their own magickal properties.

ALDER: resurrection, rebirth, fire.

APPLE: healing, prosperity, love, peace, happiness, youth.

ASH: healing, protection, sea magick.

BIRCH: new beginnings and births, fertility, purifications, protection, blessings.

BLACKTHORN: bad luck, strife, unexpected changes, death, wounding, curses.

CEDAR: purification, prosperity, longevity; represents the earth and spirituality.

ELDER: healing, love, protection, prosperity; used to make magickal wands.

ELM: primordial female powers, protection.

FIR: youth, vitality; used in prosperity magick.

HAWTHORN: female sexuality, cleansing, marriage, love, protection; a magickal tool.

HAZEL: fertility, divination, marriage, protection, reconciliation; used to make wands.

HOLLY: protection.

OAK: healing, strength, longevity.

PINE: immortality, fertility, health, prosperity; represents the earth.

ROWAN: protection, healing, strength; represents fire.

WILLOW: moon and wishing magick, healing, protection, enchantments; represents water.

YEW: immortality, rebirth, protection, longevity, change, divinity, strength.

TREE INCANTATION

Sit against a tree trunk and breathe
Seek the magick within and believe
For these wisdom keepers will draw you in
Secrets to share where the veil is thin
Magickally charged; meditation awaits
Root into the ground to now meet the fates.

MONTHS

JANUARY

Olde, frost, birch, cold moon

Letting go of the past and invoking the new

The month of January brings the energy of a new start as the calendar year begins. In the northern hemisphere the cold, hard earth remains steeped in deep magick and mystery, nurturing and restoring all that resides within it and offering comfort from the hardships the glacial callousness of winter brings. The goddess is in her crone phase but she is beginning to fade as the promise of new life beckons, and the days are getting longer since her deathly reign of winter and the solstice at Yule. This is a time of a slow awakening for all of nature and to look at setting different goals as you leave old regrets behind and make fresh resolutions through intention, ritual and spells to assist you through the coming months and warmer days.

It's time to take the first brave steps of authenticity towards the magickal freedom of embracing the witch within, to stop hesitating and hiding in the shadows. Bid farewell to negativity, control and disempowerment and embrace the lessons of the past, as the door closes on yesteryear and brighter experiences await. The crone offers you rebirth and transformation as you follow the wheel of the year and the magick of the old ways.

GODDESS: **Danu (Celtic/Irish)**, first great mother, earth goddess, cosmic triple goddess.

CRONE: transformation, dreams, clarity, wisdom, alchemical magick.

MOON MAGICK

The olde moon is a mystical artist that shines its shimmering light to reflect upon January's cold, hard earth. While the mother fuels this moon phase, the goddess is also in her crone aspect at this barren time of year. The olde moon highlights the path you are to take as you cross the threshold into a new year and consider what could be in store for you. Be assured that the Fates preside over the days and months ahead and that as you put your focus and intentions into new resolutions you are supported to dream your dreams. It is time to make decisions, to claim who you are and become it, for the best version of you waits to emerge as you follow the wheel of the year and embrace the magick of the old ways.

OLDE MOON

Olde moon shines upon the frost
Barren promises, old life lost
Bid farewell to yesterday
Resolutions light the way
This moon magick is said and done
So mote it be, with harm to none.

NEW YEAR SPELL

While holding a black tourmaline crystal
to ground and protect you, say:

New year vexed with trouble and strife
Follow the old ways, inject magick in life
Each moon phase stirs the witch within
Freedom expressed, let the new year begin
Fleeting shadows traverse witchy moon
Mystery and magick transpires very soon
Black tourmaline crystal, place upon feet
For grounding, protection against ruin, deceit
Follow the path of the ancient old ways
Invoking mystique throughout modern days
Create sacred space, let mystery enter
Triple goddess calls to represent her
Upon your altar, statues place
Maiden, mother, crone: all present to face
Embrace the path of ancient rite
Bathe under a full moon, immersed in the light
Draw down the moon and welcome the year
Empowerment beckons with nothing to fear.

Bury the black tourmaline in the
earth under the light of the moon to
restore, recharge and reclaim your
magick and power as a witch.

1 Monday

Between 40,000 to 50,000 executions occurred after witch hunts between 1450 and 1750. Not all witch hunts were recorded, so an accurate number of executions cannot be arrived at.

2 Tuesday

3 Wednesday

4 Thursday

Third quarter moon · Doreen Valiente (1922-99), mother of modern witchcraft, United Kingdom.

5 Friday

Barbara Meiklejohn-Free (1957-), high priestess, highland seer and occultist, United Kingdom.

6 Saturday

7 Sunday

8 Monday

Samuel Liddell MacGregor Mathers (1854–1918), co-founder of the Hermetic Order of the Golden Dawn, London, United Kingdom.

9 Tuesday

10 Wednesday

11 Thursday

New moon · The trial of the Basque witches began in January 1609 in Logroño, Spain.

12 Friday

13 Saturday

14 Sunday

RITUAL MAGICK

Focus your new resolutions into a white
candle, then light it and let it safely burn
down. Take a piece of material from
what has gone before, focus on all you
wish to release from the past and drown
the material in a bowl of water. Say:

Resolutions set me free
Material holds past energy
Submerge in water, hold it down.
Allow the old to finally drown.

ARNICA: RECOVERY

All forlorn, extremely bruised
So sore, in pain and feeling used
Give yourself some time to rest
My remedy restores your zest
This magick is worked, with harm to none
So mote it be; there, it is done.

KITCHEN WISDOM

ARNICA: if you've been struggling to make a comeback you may still be reeling from the blow you received. This knock has set you back somewhat and you may be wondering when life will return to normal. When you're feeling bruised and hurt and are in desperate need of some urgent TLC, convalescence is key to giving yourself time to mend and recuperate.

Not having control over the symptoms that are plaguing you can be more than frustrating, so allow me to assist in gently supporting you in your recovery process.

My rich source of manganese will facilitate your healing of any traumatic injuries, including bruises and sprains, as well as your bruised soul. Take me as a cardiac tonic and I will support your weak and weary heart. Stop trying to go it alone; instead, rest in the comfort of knowing that I will effectively nurse you to the full recovery you've been wishing for.

----○----

WITCHY RECIPE

This arnica salve is great for sprains, bruises, pain and inflammation. Into a double boiler add ¼ cup of tightly packed dried arnica flowers and ½ cup of carrier oil and simmer the mixture for 1 hour. Strain the flowers into a heat-safe glass container. Add 1 tablespoon of yellow beeswax pellets to the strained arnica oil and place it back in the double boiler. Once the pellets have melted, stir the mixture and pour it into the container with the flowers. Cool before using. For a firmer salve, add more beeswax during the preparation.

15 Monday

16 Tuesday

17 Wednesday

18 Thursday

First quarter moon.

19 Friday

In Valais, Switzerland 367 people were condemned for practising witchcraft from 1428 to 1448.

20 Saturday

21 Sunday

22 Monday

In Trier, Germany 368 people were condemned for practising witchcraft from 1581 to 1593.

23 Tuesday

24 Wednesday

Theoris of Lemnos (fourth century BCE), Greek witch and folk healer, was executed.

25 Thursday

Full moon.

26 Friday

27 Saturday

28 Sunday

Agnes Sampson, midwife, (died 1591) was strangled then burned as a witch in 1591 in Royal Mile, Edinburgh. Her trial was the first of all the witch trials to come in Scotland.

MAGICK AND MYSTERY

The magick and mystery of the old ways grants you access to the dimensions of the invisible realms, for the pull of your heart bids you follow the path of natural magick. As fleeting shadows cross the witch's moon, see through sorceress eyes and never fear your path. Instead, you must believe in your own super-witch powers, for the magick of the old ways runs through your veins and is testament to the wise ones who walked the path of the craft before you. It is time to trust in mystery and liberate the witch within, as you set free those who have been disempowered through example. Hold your head up high in witchy defiance and walk tall in wisdom and knowing as an advocate of the old ways.

FEBRUARY

Ice, snow, rowan, quickening moon

A time of purification and hope

After the harshness of winter, this is a time of emergence as new shoots appear from the ground, early flowers begin to blossom and the start of the renewal of life can be witnessed. Daylight hours finally become noticeably longer and the birth of the very first lambs as the ewes start to lactate is celebrated. It was an important time for our ancestors as fresh milk once again became available, meaning the difference between life and death after the cold, harsh scarcity of winter.

IMBOLC: 1 February

GODDESS: **Bridget (Irish/Celtic)**, new life, hope, growth.

MAIDEN: innocence, purity, seeding the dream.

~ IMBOLC ~
First signs of new growth

At Imbolc it is traditional to pour fresh milk on the ground to honour Mother Earth and ensure fertility for the coming season. In agriculture this is when seeds are planted and signs of flowers such as snowdrops and crocuses starting to grow can be seen. Imbolc is a time of purification in preparation for the coming year and is portrayed as the young virgin maiden aspect of the Celtic triple goddess. She is the young girl awakening to womanhood just as nature begins its fertility cycle and offers us new life and fresh beginnings.

This is the time to seed your new ideas, to make plans and begin creative projects that will grow into fruition through the warmer months to come. As nature starts to wake up it's time to plant and seed your wishes and desires, to awaken and create different dreams and goals.

IMBOLC INCANTATION

'neath a layer of soft white snow
Doth a single flower grow
The goddess stands in maiden form
Shining through this very dawn
New fruits stir her virgin womb
Awakening from winter's tomb
She calls to you to be free
To explore each possibility
For now is when to seed your dreams
No matter how hard and tough life seems
They will come true; it's time to trust
Be one with nature, don't fight or thrust
Take the cup she offers you
That's filled with milk from a ewe
Embrace the year through open eyes
Magick awaits; nature tells no lies.

29 Monday

30 Tuesday
The persecution of witches in Rome continued until the late fourth century CE.

31 Wednesday

1 Thursday
Imbolc · Persecution of the Cathars in France around 1450 for witchcraft and heresy.

2 Friday
Third quarter moon.

3 Saturday

4 Sunday

5 Monday

Janet Horne was the last woman in the United Kingdom to be legally executed for witchcraft, in 1727.

6 Tuesday

7 Wednesday

8 Thursday

Éliphas Lévi Zahed, greatest occultist of the 19th century.

9 Friday

Super new moon.

10 Saturday

11 Sunday

WITCH'S WISDOM

The triple goddess in her shining maiden form invites you back in at a much deeper level to unleash the innocent part of you within, the part that nourishes and fills you and reminds you not to take things so seriously. Your inner child is that beautiful, innocent, creative, imaginative part of you that just wants to have fun, to lighten up and splash about in puddles. For now, February beckons you to play under the soft glow of the maiden. Just like the driven snow, she is pure and offers a clean slate, especially if you've been caught out through naivety, gullibility and lack of experience. It's time to get back to simplicity, to release rigidity and ideas of perfection. Instead, forge your true identity and honour your maiden qualities as you discover the pleasure of new exploration, adventure and excitement. The maiden is the young girl at the start of her fertility cycle, awakening to the delicious promise of womanhood, pure and virtuous and with all the fresh offerings of spring.

GODDESS INCANTATION

The goddess stands in maiden form
Shining through this very dawn
Virtue found within, so deep
Arise and stir from deepest sleep
This magick is worked with harm to none
So mote it be; there, it is done.

WITCHERY

The maiden is the young aspect of the triple goddess. She is the joy of new life, and has the innocence and purity of lambs. She is the lack of worry and carefree stance of youth, the inexperienced virgin who innocently allures and enchants through her naive purity and feminine independence. Associated with spring, she offers new beginnings and the birth of fresh projects, creativity, sexual innocence and discovery.

12   Monday

13   Tuesday

14   Wednesday

15   Thursday

16   Friday
First quarter moon · Pamela Colman Smith (1878–1951), occultist and artist of the Rider-Waite tarot.

17   Saturday

18   Sunday

19 Monday

More than 5,000 members of the Bacchus cult were executed between 182 and 184 BCE by the Roman senate for practising witchcraft at the ecstatic rites of Dionysus.

20 Tuesday

21 Wednesday

22 Thursday

La Voisin (1640–80), French fortune teller, sorceress and commissioned poisoner; burned at the stake. Sybil Leek (1917–82), witch, occult author and astrologer.

23 Friday

24 Saturday

Full moon · Penumbral lunar eclipse.

25 Sunday

Forty-five men and 85 women suspected of sorcery were executed during the reign of Tibetus Claudius, from 41 to 54 CE.

MOON MAGICK

Magickal effects and intensification abounds when the supermoon rises on 9 February. Can you not feel the force as the powerful boost of light grows bigger and brighter? At this time your sorcery is at its optimum, so there is no better time to cast spells and harness ritual magick. Allow the moonlight to flood your senses as you look inward to determine how best to proceed. The ruling lunar-charged skies present you with powers of extremity, so take advantage of this influential super presence by tapping into and harnessing your own personal power. As the full moon heightens unseen experiences within, feel it prime the energies all around as you embrace your talents and witchy gifts. Don't buy into competition; there is enough of the good stuff to go round. Instead, it's your chance to truly shine like a cornucopia of plenty, as you grow stronger in ethics and abilities as a witch and become supercharged under the abundant energy of the supermoon.

SUPERMOON: ABUNDANCE

Supermoon heightens this very eve
Power and force entwined, doth weave
Harness, for plentiful magick is charged
More than sufficient, richly recharged
This moon magick is said and done
So mote it be, with harm to none.

SUPERMOON RITUALS

To raise power and attract abundance during the supermoon: chant powerful incantations; dance skyclad around a huge fire to expend energy; place citrine crystals outside to catch the moon's light and ensure prosperity; scratch intentions of abundance into a purple candle and safely burn it down; write down all you wish to attract; and engage in energy healing.

LEAP YEAR MAGICK

Witches understand that leap years are needed to ensure the earth's revolutions, and work with highly charged liminal energy to increase good fortune and any magick that their heart desires. Traditionally associated with love, romance and super empowerment, ladies can propose marriage to their beloveds on this day instead of being asked. As 29 February is a hidden day shrouded from our world for three years at a time, witches seize the chance to utilise its powerful charge to find or locate items or something deep within that is hidden or lost.

The earth nurtures and restores all that resides in and on her. By working a little earth magick you can be assured that whatever has been misplaced shall soon be uncovered.

FINDING SPELL

Light a black candle and face north. Write the name of a lost item or something you wish to find on a piece of paper and say:

Upon this day may power abound
Highly charged spells for what's lost to be found
There's something I'm missing and just cannot find
I picture the item within my clear mind
To find and retrieve from the vision I see
I ask it's return for safekeeping to me.
Release and free that which is mine
So I can reclaim it, all in good time
Vanished, misplaced, now soon to appear
This magick is done upon a leap year.

Blow out the candle, fold the piece of
paper four times and bury it in the earth.
Your lost item will be returned in an
unexpected and magickal way.

26 Monday

27 Tuesday
Comte de Saint Germain (1712-84), Hungarian alchemist and philosopher.

28 Wednesday

29 Thursday
Leap year! · The first warrants were issued at the Salem witch trials on 29 February 1692.

1 Friday
First Witchcraft Act in England in 1542; the instigator was Henry VIII.

2 Saturday

3 Sunday
Third quarter moon.

MARCH

Moon of winds, storm, ash, worm and crow moon

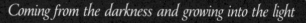

Coming from the darkness and growing into the light

In like a lion and out like a lamb, the winds of change welcome in this wild month, which brings hope of warmer days to come. The energy at this waxing time of year becomes expansive as the light grows strong enough to defeat the dark, and the natural world comes alive as the sun gains strength with the promise of longer and warmer days. As the goddess in her maiden form walks across the land, all of nature wakes up to the fulfilled promises made at Imbolc as she breathes new life into the world. Spring has sprung!

OSTARA: 20 March

GODDESS: **Ēostre/Ostara (Anglo/Germanic),** of spring, fertility, renewal, fruitfulness.

MAIDEN: the dark of the old aligns with new light, signs of growth, creative power.

~ OSTARA ~

Alignment of the natural world

Ostara heralds the spring equinox, a time of balance between light and dark and a day of equilibrium. When you are aligned with the natural world you can embrace and honour the new creative power that is stirring throughout nature.

Ostara is a time for honouring new life and is the festival that was borrowed from age-old traditions to become Easter; think hatched eggs, baby chicks, moon-gazing hares and all the fresh promises of spring. Call upon the spirits of the air to enhance your creativity and meditation abilities and to stimulate your mind as you light incense and a yellow candle and face the direction of east. This is a great time for fertility as air blows you in the direction of new beginnings, so throw caution to the wind and watch as your visions manifest into reality.

OSTARA INCANTATION

Celebrate the stirring of spring
Natural balance doth it bring
Claim that of which it represents:
New life, growth and expectance
Seeds planted in nature's tomb
Incubate within her womb
Symbolic hares upon the lawn
Herald the goddess of the dawn
And from the east the sun doth rise
Shining bright across the skies
The goddess works behind the scenes
To manifest your goals and dreams
Await and trust now; 'tis the key
For life will bloom most readily.

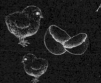

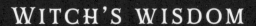

WITCH'S WISDOM

Steeped in mystery and superstition, our healing history is shared among the hedgerows – for we witches are a brave and hardy sort who have survived over centuries past as healers and herbalists. Hidden recipes of natural brews and tinctures have cured and healed, although many of us have been killed for secrets as powerful as these. Healing knowledge and folk medicine are much sort-after enigmas, taken from the old unwritten ways after being handed down orally by witches of olde. The witchy healer cures ailments and suffering through herbal teas, tinctures and potions, all brewed up in a cauldron, of course. Discovering curative roots, herbs, spices and plants combines hearth and home with pure witchy healing magick. As a natural healer yourself, use and trust your inner instincts as you seek and draw from the power of nature to make therapeutic remedies and cures through infusions, poultices and salves. Choose natural ingredients wisely and learn well from the plant teachers, who share with you their restorative wisdom.

CURES/REMEDIES

Come heal discomfort, illness, pain
Remedies to ease the strain
Herbal cures prevent decay
Infections, flu: begone, away!
This magick is worked with harm to none
So mote it be; there, it is done.

4 Monday

Lilias Adie (1640-1704), Scottish witch, died in prison before her sentence was passed. She is the only known witch in Scotland to have a grave, at Torryburn Bay in intertidal mud and with a heavy stone doorstep on top.

5 Tuesday

6 Wednesday

Laurie Cabot (1933-), high priestess and occultist, Salem, United States.

7 Thursday

8 Friday

9 Saturday

Between the 4th and 6th centuries CE more than 1,000 witches were persecuted and expelled from the Huns, a nomadic tribe.

10 Sunday

Super new moon.

11   Monday

12   Tuesday

Hypatia (350–415 CE), ancient philosopher and astronomer; murdered by a Christian mob that accused her of practising witchcraft.

13   Wednesday

14   Thursday

15   Friday

16   Saturday

17   Sunday

First quarter moon.

WITCHY TIP

The goddess calls you to take refuge in the darkness of her womb, and there she will nurture you as she stirs her cauldron until you are well rested and healed.

WITCHY RECIPE

This tincture tonic is a great cough medicine for relieving the effects of influenza and colds.
Fill a pint-sized jar with ½ cup of either fresh leaves and root of echinacea or dried leaves. Pour boiling water over the herb to draw out the properties until the jar is half full. Add enough apple cider vinegar to fill the jar and stir. Strain the mixture through cheesecloth and store in dark bottles, shaking daily.

Dip a finger into your magickal potion and place your finger upon your heart to transform and inspire healing. So mote it be.

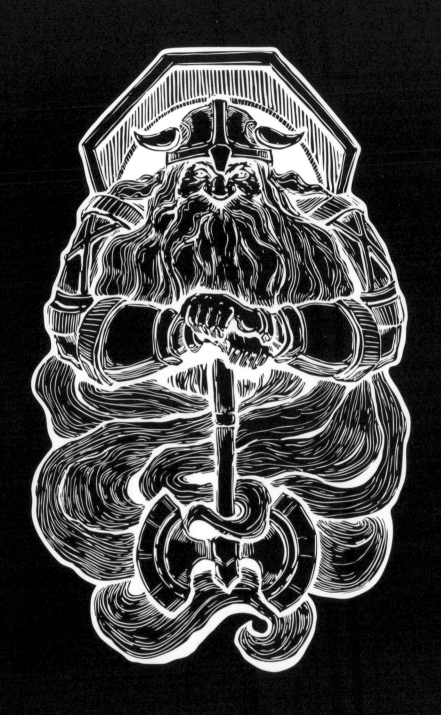

FAMILIAR'S MESSAGE

DWARF: cunning, resilience and acceptance are my tools when it comes to highly effective magickal work. The ability to see alternative solutions when you're confronted with a problem is pure witchy resourcefulness, and a tricky situation calls you to be quick-witted, clever and bright if you want results. As you harness the ability to process information emotionally as well as intellectually, I can help you get the job done against all odds. My intimate knowledge and robust focus is instrumental when it comes to working with the craft, and I will teach you how to hone less admirable qualities such as pride, greed and stubbornness to get what you want even when things look impossible. As you become more resistant to outside influence I will gift you two magickal stones. Whenever you're feeling cursed, hexed or in a crisis, choose wisely between strength and invisibility in your quest to overcome difficulties.

RESOURCEFUL DWARVES

Metals, crystals, stones aligned
Resources extracted and mined
Runic symbols etched on tools
Ingenious, wise and not for fools.

WITCHY TIP

As skilled craftsmen and metalsmiths, dwarves support the Norse gods and aid them with their wisdom and cleverness. Resistant to basic magick, dwarves work magick manipulation through runes.

Inscribe the runic symbol for protection onto a black obsidian crystal for the safe guardianship of the dwarves against chaos magick.

18 Monday

Manly Palmer Hall (1901-90), mystic and astrologer.

19 Tuesday

20 Wednesday

Ostara, spring equinox.

21 Thursday

22 Friday

23 Saturday

In the 1590s, the Scottish King James I's fear of witchcraft and black magick caused thousands of witches, mostly women, to be burned and tortured. He believed there was a witchcraft conspiracy against him that threatened his reign.

24 Sunday

Penumbral lunar eclipse.

KITCHEN WITCHERY

MINT: when you just can't think straight or when your brain feels fogged, you can rely on my refreshing magick to clear your mind, enhance your intellect and provide mental clarity. My cooling qualities will soothe and calm you from the stressful effects of overthinking as well as physical ailments such as sore throats and indigestion. Allow me to sharpen your words so they are fully understood as I sweeten your breath. Add my leaves to running bath water to indulge in a rejuvenating soak, and as you relax your mind place fresh peppermint leaves on your forehead to relieve nervous headaches. Soon the visions you've been asking for will become lucid, and you will gain a greater understanding as you trust in the messages of your inner witch.

MINT: CLARITY

Understanding is hard to find
I'll breathe my power through your mind
Add my leaves to pot of tea
Then sip and you will better see
This magick is worked, with harm to none
So mote it be; there, it is done.

WITCHY RECIPE

This paste is good for fresh breath, spots and odour on your hands after cooking. Add 1 cup of freshly chopped mint leaves to a saucepan, cover with spring or filtered water and bring to a boil. Remove from the heat and allow the mixture to cool. Place ½ teaspoon of sunflower oil and ½ cup of cornstarch in a separate saucepan and stir until smooth. Add the mint to the oil/cornstarch mix, then stir over medium heat until it comes to a boil. Remove from the heat and place the paste in a container.

CLARITY SPELL

Hold a clear quartz
crystal sphere and say:

Unclear, foggy, just can't think
Lucidity is on the brink
Peer into the crystal shores
Quartz reveals a block of fear
Place gently upon third eye
To clear the mind and detoxify
Clarity shines throughout the dark
Sharpened focus makes the mark
Rich inner world springs to mind
Deep hidden treasures now to find.

Plant the quartz into the
earth so that your goals and
ideas can grow into fruition
over the coming months.

MARCH

25 Monday
Full moon.

26 Tuesday
Zhang Liang executed for treason and witchcraft in 646 CE.

27 Wednesday

28 Thursday

29 Friday
Granny Boswell (1813-1909), well-known local witch in Cornwall; married the king of the witches.

30 Saturday

31 Sunday

APRIL

Growing, alder, seed moon

Growth, planting and connecting with the magick of nature

The fresh, light rain of April brings with it new ideas and inspiration. This is a great time for wishes and magick as the earth springs forth and faeries tend to and nurture their wards, the newly growing flowers. For thousands of years witches and healers have worked alongside the power of the fae, who have shared their ancient knowledge of healing herbs, cures and ointments with those who visit their mystical world. As a magickal energy of growth surrounds you the fae are poised to support you, as heartfelt wishes reflect your thoughts and good intentions. The fae are the guardians of nature who remind you that magick is everywhere and in everything, so go outside and discover it! Enjoy every precious moment, knowing and appreciating that you are totally blessed as you feel the faery witch within stir deeply.

GODDESS: **Cordelia (Celtic/British)**, faery queen of flowers, faeries, beauty, wishes.

MAIDEN: renewing of spirit, inhaling fresh air, the fragrance of spring flowers.

WITCH'S WISDOM

A witch has the ability to point her witchy finger to reward, punish or control another with a blessing, curse or glamour trick. However, don't be caught up in illusion, for looks can be deceiving; everything is not what it seems when it comes to working with the glamour of charms and enchantment. Over the centuries, muggles have sought out witches for their dark secrets and alluring abilities to change an outcome, so as you weave a little charm magick open your eyes with an ancient ointment that works to reveal all manner of disguise, giving you charmed access to the enchanting magickal realms.

WITCHY TIP

Whenever a faery wishes to be seen by humankind they use faery magick to slow down their vibration. Sometimes they deliberately enhance their shining beauty to pull us in with all sorts of faery enchantment, charms and other illusions. This magick, which is called 'glamour', is not real in the world we live in. Faeries have used glamour to shapeshift into animals, to appear shorter or taller than they really are and to appear in human form as we expect to see them.

1 Monday

Second Witchcraft Act in England in 1563; the instigator was Elizabeth I.

2 Tuesday

Third quarter moon.

3 Wednesday

4 Thursday

5 Friday

6 Saturday

7 Sunday

Anne Pedersdotter (ca 1530-90) Norwegian witch, burned to death.

8 Monday
Total solar eclipse and super new moon.

9 Tuesday

10 Wednesday

11 Thursday

12 Friday
Raven Grimassi (1951–2019), high priest, occultism and wiccan; popularised Stregheria, the root of witchcraft.

13 Saturday
William Quan Judge (1851-96), occultist, mystic and founder of the Theosophical Society.

14 Sunday

GLAMOUR
INCANTATION

Manipulation, blessing, curse
Glamour trick or something worse
Bewitching spells that work a charm
Enchanting words to heal or harm
Charm magick is worked with harm to none
So mote it be; there, it is done.

WITCHY TIP

If you've been under
the spell of someone
whose charm has caused
you to behave in a
different way than usual,
it's time to break the
illusion and walk away
from manipulation.

WITCHERY

Charms are carriers of energy and power that can be used in spells or placed into objects for magickal effects. To begin, a witch raises the energy to place within it the power of intent. Visualise a brightly coloured ball of light in your hands and see its energy growing until it feels strong. Focus on your intentions, through incantation if you wish. Imagine your charm absorbing the light until it radiates and pulsates with newly charged magickal intention, then place it into a spell or object.

Keep your charms regularly charged by repeating invocations and your witchy intentions for their purposes.

FAERY ENCHANTMENT SPELL

Doubts begone, release all fright
Relax and see through sacred sight
Faery oil upon third eye
Senses soar as you fly high
Flash of light, orbs to catch
Faeries seen through strike of match
As candles burn to show the way
Betwixt the worlds of you and fae.

15 Monday

First quarter moon. During the Channel Island witch trials from 1550 to 1650 more than 100 people were accused, tortured and executed.

16 Tuesday

17 Wednesday

18 Thursday

King Olaf Tryggvason of Norway (reigned 995–1000 CE) lured more than 100 pagan magicians into his hall under false pretences and accused them of practising witchcraft. The doors were barred and they were burned; those that escaped were captured and drowned.

19 Friday

20 Saturday

21 Sunday

22 Monday

23 Tuesday
Ursulines de Jésus (??) burned to death in Brazil in 1754 for practising witchcraft.

24 Wednesday
Full moon.

25 Thursday

26 Friday

27 Saturday

28 Sunday

FAERY CHARM

Hold a cleansed piece of clear quartz crystal upon your
third eye chakra to open up your spiritual sight.

FAERY GLAMOUR

Faeries of beauty, please help me to be
Dazzling and gorgeous for all life to see
Share, if you will, your tips of the trade
Make me pretty and perfect, as you are all made
Desires, now shared, I wish to ignite
My passionate dreams so that I might
Attract beauty and love into my world
May deep the love mystery now be unfurled
To bring about romance, kisses and laughter
And be of my heart, happily ever after.

MAY

Hare, milk, bright, willow moon

A celebration of nature in full bloom

The merry month of May is a celebration of when the energies of nature are at their strongest. All of life is bursting with potent fertility, the goddess is seeded by the god and we witness the conception of new life bursting forth into full bloom at the start of the summer months to come.

BELTANE: 1 May

GODDESS: **Blodeuwedd (Celtic/Welsh)**, 'flower face', springtime flowers, new warmth.

MAIDEN: in her fullness, sexuality, sensuality, passion, vitality, consummation.

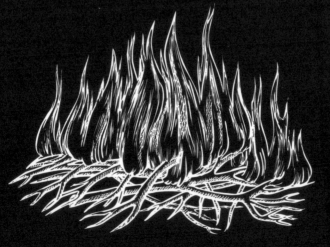

~ BELTANE ~

The maiden has reached her fullness and is the manifestation of growth, sexuality, sensuality, passion, vitality and consummation

Beltane is an age-old, yearly pagan celebration that continues to this day. Villagers gather to eat together and sup ale as they are treated to traditional Morris dancing and a May queen is chosen, and local children weave ribbons in and out as they dance around a decorated maypole. This represents the rituals once held to promote fertility for livestock and people alike.

Traditionally, Beltane is a time of the blending of energies of the feminine and masculine to celebrate the sacredness of sexuality. The goddess takes on the god as her lover in order to give birth to the full bloom of nature during the summer months to come. Beltane marks the return of full life and nature is fully honoured in the fresh bright flowers, grasses and leaves that have started to push through. It is an abundant time of year; think maypoles – a phallic symbol that represents the potency of the gods – May queens, flower garlands, handfasting and hawthorn (known as the May tree) and the lord and lady of the Greenwood church.

Beltane is celebrated as a fire festival to honour the Celtic sun god Bel. Great fires blazed from the hilltops as a sign of protection and others were lit for couples to leap over hand in hand before running into the woods to consummate their union. It's a time when the goals that were set at the beginning of the year come to fruition, and when projects take off and relationships bloom. Seeds are sown at Beltane and the goddess from her union with her consort gives birth to goals, dreams and ideas, which spring into reality and continue to grow and blossom into fruition.

BELTANE INCANTATION

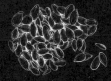

With fires lit across the land
A couple leaps while hand in hand
To mark their union and this rite
For they know tonight's the night!
As they run through darkened wood
And find a grassy glade, they should
Remember well of who's around
For bands of faeries all surround
The couple as they consummate,
The faeries cheer and seal the fate
Of plants and flowers, shrubs and trees
While the god's upon his knees
Impregnating the mother to be
From sowing deep his natural seed
And so in time the goddess will birth
The magick that is nature on this earth.

WITCH'S WISDOM

As witches heal from the burning times and the persecutions of yesteryear there still remains a deep affinity with the projective and transformative energy of fire, for a lit flame plays a hallowed part in magick, ceremony and ritual. The element of fire illuminates the path of the witch, who manipulates the power of the flame for its warmth, life force and destructive nature through spell work and healing purpose. Allow fire's essence to purify your body and spark your spirit. Igniting the inner flame of passion in your heart with strength and desire will incite your life's work and spice up your love life! Fire is not to be feared: it's your ticket to full empowerment, fuelling your ability to kindle your true light with full might, vitality and vigour and ignite your magickal power.

29 Monday

Titus Livius recorded that 170 women were executed as witches for causing an epidemic illness in Rome in 331 BCE.

30 Tuesday

1 Wednesday

Beltane, May Day · Third quarter moon.

2 Thursday

Third Witchcraft Act in England in 1604; the instigator was James I.

3 Friday

4 Saturday

5 Sunday

MAY

6 Monday

Margaret Read (??) burned at the stake in 1590 in King's Lynn, Norfolk.

7 Tuesday

8 Wednesday

New moon.

9 Thursday

Isobel Gowdie, Scottish witch, confessed under duress in 1662 to practising witchcraft.

10 Friday

11 Saturday

12 Sunday

PASSION INCANTATION

Ignite the flame, let the magick begin
Passion fuels the desires within
Feeling the heat, candles to light
Spice up my love life, for tonight is the night!
Beltane magick is now said and done
So mote it be, with harm to none.

RENEWAL RITUAL

Fire walk skyclad under a full moon for empowerment and transformation.
Allow a candle flame to burn down to seal spell. Engage in fire scrying by staring at a lit flame or fire without blinking. Watch pictures take shape or close your eyes and see the fire in your mind, pushing pictures down into your heart to connect with the fire's essence.

WITCHY TIP

Belief in both your tools and yourself when performing any candle magick ritual is critical for success.
Scratch intentions into candle wax with a pin then anoint the wax with sacred oils for purity of power. Allow the candle flame to safely burn all the way down to seal a spell.

KITCHEN WITCHERY

CORIANDER: like the element of fire, you seem to be indestructible! When you allow nothing to stand in your way and laugh in the face of any obstacles and challenges, good news relating to a project you're working on will have the impact you've been hoping for. In fact, your efforts will be acknowledged for quite some time as you make your mark in the world and achieve everlasting success.

Don't give in to your fears of change or endings. Instead, add me to your diet so I can enhance your mental alertness and spiritual motivation while your body achieves optimum health and longevity. This also relates to affairs of the heart, especially while in the energies of Beltane. You can be sure of long-lasting and meaningful relationships when I appear as you add 19 of my seeds crushed to a powder to red wine and drink it with your beloved under the May new moon on Wednesday, 8 May.

CORIANDER: IMMORTALITY

Don't back down, you're flying high
The only limit is the sky
Longevity of each endeavour
Eat of me and live forever!
This magick is worked, with harm to none
So mote it be; there, it is done.

WITCHY RECIPE

This juice is a great detoxer for fatigue, mouth ulcers and blood sugar. Mince a handful of fresh coriander leaves and add them to a saucepan of filtered water. Boil for 10 minutes, then strain the juice and leave it to cool. If you wish you can mix in some lemon or salt. Drink or gargle as necessary.

13 Monday

In the first century CE, 80 women were executed for practising witchcraft in Ashkelon, in Canaan in the Middle East.

14 Tuesday

15 Wednesday

First quarter moon.

16 Thursday

17 Friday

18 Saturday

Cassandra Latham-Jones (??) was the first person in the United Kingdom to register her work as a witch with the Inland Revenue Department, in 1996.

19 Sunday

20 Monday

21 Tuesday

22 Wednesday

23 Thursday

Full moon · Kenneth Grant (1924–2011), ceremonial magician and an advocate of the
Thelemic religion.

24 Friday

25 Saturday

26 Sunday

FIRE PASSION SPELL

To invite the power of fire into your life connect
with the mighty elemental salamander, who ignites
the flame and fires up inner passion.

Face the direction of south and light a red
candle, then gaze into the flame and say:

Salamanders, spirits of fire
Bring me your courage and all I desire
Ignite the flame of passion within
So I can connect with the strength of the djinn
With honour, respect, I call upon you
Please help me to work my life purpose through
Extinguish the dark that blacks out the light
So I am released of fears and my plight
Allow the fire to ravage through me
To purify, cleanse and set me free
I am of power, this I now know
As I become the sacred glow
Dear beings of light, of summer and sun
With my heart I give thanks. There, it is done.

27 Monday

Nicholas II of Russia had a great fascination with occult magick and introduced it into the imperial court. He was connected to Rasputin, a mystic and seer who was murdered in December 1916. A year later the tsar abdicated his throne.

28 Tuesday

29 Wednesday

30 Thursday

Third quarter moon · Joan of Arc (ca 1412–31), visionary; burned for heresy and practising witchcraft.

31 Friday

1 Saturday

Fourth Witchcraft Act in England in 1735, instigated by parliament. The act abolished the hunting and execution of witches in the United Kingdom, as it was made a crime for any person to claim another person had magickal powers or was guilty of being a practising witch.

2 Sunday

JUNE

Moon of horses, hawthorn, strawberry moon

Glorifying the full strength and light of the sun

June is busting out all over as we celebrate the full bloom of roses, honeysuckle and warmer weather. Named after the Roman goddess of marriage, Juno, sunny June sees the start of the wedding season and a June bride is considered to be lucky. June is also the halfway stage of the growing season for farmers, a traditional midpoint between planting and harvesting. The goddess is now the mother, and the sun god is at the height of his virility and life-giving power. Celebrations of fullness, expansiveness and achievements are awash with joy as the light reaches its peak and the longest day and shortest night of the wheel of the year are enjoyed.

LITHA: 21 June

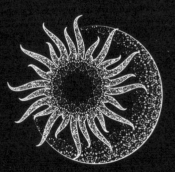

GODDESS: Áine (Celtic/Irish), faery queen of summer, growth, love, luck, magick.

MOTHER: in her full power, strength.

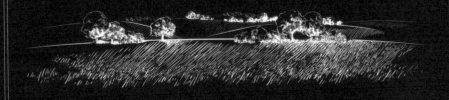

~ LITHA ~

Empowerment, celebration of light and full strength of the sun

This is the month that celebrates the sun festival known as Litha, or the summer solstice, when the sun is at its highest point in the sky and is at its strongest. It is a time of intensification, of focus, development and determination as we connect with the sun to become stronger and claim our full self-power in celebration, honour and ritual. Those who are not aware of such connotation may still, albeit unwittingly, worship the sun in other ways, for they partake in outdoor parties and barbecues and top up their tans during hot and sunny days. Celtic tradition honoured through tales and legends tells of a great battle that plays out at this time of year between the mighty holly king and the majestic oak king. At the summer solstice the holly king wins supreme and stands proud through to winter, until at Yule he is cut down in his prime when the oak king wins and presides over the coming months until their next battle at Litha.

This is a time of year when you can tap into midsummer magick, as the veil between the worlds is thin; think Titania, Oberon, faery spells and faery rings of mushrooms, toadstools and flowers where those with an open heart are invited in to connect with the natural magick of the fae.

MIDSUMMER INVOCATION

As I enter within this magickal ring
My heart is open and ready to sing
Songs of the wood, words of the fae
Who guide me in and show me the way
I call on the magick of Midsummer's Eve
Whose mystic and mystery together doth weave
May power bestow me this very night
As I share my found gifts, for 'tis only right
With arms outstretched to the magickal ones
I give honour and thanks. So now it is done.

3   Monday

4   Tuesday

Since 2021 witch-hunts have made a resurgence in the Democratic Republic of Congo.
Eight women were burned to death or lynched in September, and between June and September
there were 324 accusations recorded of people practising witchcraft.

5   Wednesday

6   Thursday

New moon · Alex Sanders (1926–88), occultist, high priest and founder of Alexandrian wicca.

7   Friday

Swein Macdonald (1931–2003), highland seer, mystic and occultist.

8   Saturday

9   Sunday

10 Monday

The hanging of witches begins at Gallows Hill, Salem, Massachusetts. Bridget Bishop was the first witch to hang, in 1692.

11 Tuesday

12 Wednesday

13 Thursday

Gerald Gardner (1884-1964), high priest and founder of Gardnerian wicca.

14 Friday

First quarter moon.

15 Saturday

Muree bin Ali bin Issa al-Asiri (??) beheaded in Saudi Arabia in 2012 for practising witchcraft.

16 Sunday

WITCH'S WISDOM

As you harness the intense power of heady June, during which the days are long and the sun is at its highest point in the sky, the moon of horses, the full moon of June, bids you to break away. Free will is your birthright, yet restriction has you tied to the fence when it comes to doing your own thing. Worrying about others or doubting your full potential could dim your wild spirit, which only wants you to run untamed and be free.

Your magickal power is eternal, so when burdens of emotional commitment suffocate the expression of your soul it's time to rise up and gallop off into the sunset. You are holding on way too tightly, and it's time to loosen the grip of control and trust your intuition whenever the odds are against you. Your best bet is to allow June's horse moon, which rises at the solstice and is packed with empowerment, to carry your heavy load and liberate the freedom of your mind as you race towards the winning line.

HORSE MOON

Horse moon's up, freedom abounds
Galloping wildly with horses and hounds
Ride through rainbows to seek, explore
Limitations of old are no more
This moon magick is said and done
So mote it be, with harm to none.

FREEDOM RITUAL

Scratch the word 'freedom' or any words of restrictions you wish to lift into the wax of a red candle and anoint the candle with cinnamon oil. Face south and light the candle.

Hold a feather and infuse your desires for freedom into it. Say:

Wishes made for liberation
Placed in feather to awaken
Thrown up high in southerly breeze
Restriction lifted, bringing ease.

WITCHY TIP

In magickal terms summer is in the direction of the south, is the time of noon and is associated with the element of fire. This season ignites your inner power, which is the bringer of passion, attraction, illumination, love, warmth, courage and strength. The sun, the greatest example of the element of fire, has always been honoured by ancient cultures including the mystical faery realm, which celebrates this giver of life throughout the fiery months of summer.

VITALITY INCANTATION

A celebration from maiden to mother
Litha and summer now offer another
Empowerment fuels through sun's ascent
In honour and ritual to reclaiming strength
This magick is worked with harm to none
So mote it be; there, it is done.

17 Monday

18 Tuesday

19 Wednesday

20 Thursday

21 Friday
Liltha, summer solstice, midsummer.

22 Saturday
Full moon.

23 Sunday

24 Monday

25 Tuesday

26 Wednesday

27 Thursday
Scott Cunningham (1956–93), author on wicca and herbalism.

28 Friday
Third quarter moon.

29 Saturday
In India women are still labelled as being witches in order to take their lands, settle scores or punish them for not accepting sexual advances. It is estimated that between 50 and 100 women are killed each year for being practising witches.

30 Sunday

SWAN'S MESSAGE

Love and romance fill the month of June with sunny blessings and marriages. Though I am true to another for life, your path may look very different now. Trust is in question when it comes to affairs of the heart, when the temptation to deceive is strong. You must employ greater honesty.; this is about being true to yourself. It takes great understanding, patience, compromise and forgiveness to maintain any meaningful relationships for a long period of time, but if done so with honesty your relationships can be the rocks that a most magickal life is built upon.

The most powerful of any relationship is the one you have with yourself. Come under my wing. Don't cheat on yourself by pretending to be something you're not or avoiding the things you need to work on from within. Be your own best life partner and anyone else you engage, in friendship, love or business, will flourish in your company.

SWAN: FIDELITY

Allegiance sworn, trust to believe
Faith in troth, hearts worn on sleeve
As temptation tests truest bond
Fidelity goes way beyond.

WITCHY TIP

Placing a swan's feather on your altar will invite love, support and healing to embrace your physical and emotional selves.

FAERY RING

To make a faery ring, make a circle by sprinkling faery dust, dried leaves, grasses, flowers and so on. Close your eyes and visualise this circle coming to life, just as mushrooms and toadstools spring up, and creating a magickal circle. Grasses and moss grow in between fungi and tiny flowers open up. Smell the sweet scent of the grass and flowers being mixed with the earthy scent of the mushrooms. Look at the perimeter of the faery ring and notice the energy that spins around it like a wall of gold, creating an energy field of magickal summer empowerment that transcends time and space.

FAERY RING INCANTATION

I create this ring in honour of the fae
And ask for protection on this Midsummer's Day
As I enter this portal of where the veil is thin
I ask that the faeries welcome me within.

JULY

Hay, thunder, mead, oak moon

———◯———

The power of summer burns brightly, intensifying passion and destiny

The month of July signifies the height of summer in all its glorious radiance, as the sun beats down upon the optimum abundance of nature's full bloom. Now is the time to enjoy the gifts of the mother goddess, for your work is done.

The magick of summer invites intense energies of lust, passion, attraction, illumination, love, sex, sun and heat, so put down your tools, have fun and enjoy the carefree days of summer. Taking a well-deserved break to rejuvenate and have some fun is essential for your well-being on all levels, but be careful not to get burned as you enjoy outdoor parties, barbecues and sunbathing during this hot, passionate month and as you worship the sun and harness the power of the element of fire.

In magickal terms, the intensity of high noon is a perfect time to cast spells as you face the direction of south. As the heat of the sun breathes renewed passion into your workings and relationships you attract the energy of abundance, awakening your spiritual kundalini energy through lust, attraction and desire as you draw down the sun's energy. As the sun greets you it highlights the path you are to take towards your destiny so you can complete your life's mission.

———◯———

GODDESS: **Étain (Celtic/Irish)**, the shining one, sun/moon goddess, lights the way on the path of transformation, towards balance, wholeness, rebirth.

MOTHER: uncovering the light and strength within, beauty, sun, love, vitality of life.

SUMMER INCANTATION

Ignite the passion of summer and know
You are the power, the sacred glow
Love and passion stirred and invoked
Abundance is yours now the fire is stoked
Lounging, bronzing in the sun
Sea salt air and having fun
Food delights, cocktails too
Take this well-earned break; for you
To be restored, take the charge
Enjoy the rest now. Bon voyage!

WITCH'S WISDOM

Whether it's your lust for life, belief in yourself or motivation, the element of fire is waiting to spice up your life!
Witches have a deep affinity with this element, for they recognise the power of a flame through spell work and connection with the ancestors. The magick of fire invokes lust, passion, attraction and love. You are being encouraged to cast aside your fear of the flame and bring more warmth into your inner world. As you invite fire into your life, allow the strength of its energy to purify and cleanse any doubts and worries that have darkened your outlook. The motivating force of fire will reignite your inner flame of passion, fuelling you so you can walk in your true light with full might, vitality and vigour and reclaim your power.

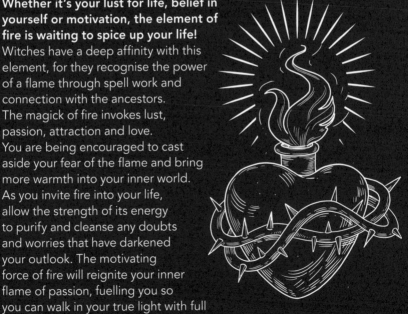

FIRE INCANTATION

Now call upon the spirit of fire
To invoke new courage and all you desire
Its strength will ravish fears and plight
And ignite the flame of passion tonight
This magic is worked, with harm to none
So mote it be; there, it is done.

GODDESS MAGICK

You are safe on this earth, nurtured within the womb of Gaia, the earth mother, the very soul of the earth. It is she who emerged from the cosmic egg at the dawn of creation and whom witches honour and revere as the source of our kind. She is fertility, stability and a giver of life, for she created and sustained us. Through the cycles of birth, fertility and sexual union and the processes of growth it is from Gaia we can learn how to be an earth mother while living on Mother Earth.

Your own challenges have created a deep and natural mothering instinct within that urges you to help many others, as a mother would help her own children. A deep process of healing and rebirth from mother's womb to earth womb will nurture and fulfil you on a very personal level. As you work closely with the goddess in her mother aspect you become ripe with expectancy, as the fruits of new projects and old labours burst forth whole and complete into the fullness of life.

MOTHER INCANTATION

Emerge from deep within her seeded womb
Fulfilment lightens darkest room
Whole and ripe, giver of life
Blessed goddess, divine wife
Mother magick is worked with harm to none
So mote it be; there, it is done.

1 Monday

Witchcraft Act in England repealed in 1951 and replaced with the Fraudulent Mediums Act.

2 Tuesday

3 Wednesday

4 Thursday

5 Friday

New moon · Lucy Cavendish (1961-), bestselling author, witch and druid.

6 Saturday

7 Sunday

JULY

8 Monday

9 Tuesday

10 Wednesday

11 Thursday

12 Friday

13 Saturday

First quarter moon · Margaret Murray (1863–1963), Egyptologist, archaeologist, occultist and folklorist; the first woman to be appointed as a lecturer in a university, in 1898. John Dee (1527–1608), court astronomer to Elizabeth I of England, occultist, alchemist and mystic.

14 Sunday

WITCHERY

The mother aspect of the triple goddess is birthed at the full moon. She bestows upon the earth abundance and gives birth to nature, having made love as the May queen with the horned god at Beltane. She is fulfilment, passion and the giver of life, as she is responsible for the flourishing season of summer and manifestation. She is the adult who is responsible and nurturing and the sustainer of life, just like the strength of the midsummer sun.

ASPECTS: ripeness, fertility, growth, fulfilment, stability, giving, nurturing, compassionate.

SEASON: summer.

COLOUR: red.

MOON PHASE: full.

KITCHEN WISDOM

NUTMEG: it's your lucky day, for when I appear in your kitchen you can be sure that your prosperity will improve for the better! This may sound too good to be true, but haven't you been asking for a change in fortune? Carry me as a charm to ensure a favourable outcome in legal matters, or in your pocket to bring you luck on your summer travels. Add me to beverages and sip of me to enhance visions through meditation, or rub a little oil onto your temples to open up your natural clairvoyant abilities. Anointing green candles with nutmeg essential oil during money spells will draw prosperity to your household, and carrying a whole nutmeg seed when gambling in card games will bring you all the luck you need to be a winner. There's no illusion, for when Lady Luck is on your side you cannot lose.

NUTMEG: LUCK

A stroke of luck, I'm here today
Good fortune favours; oh, hurray!
Hold me when you wish to win
Now take a chance; your luck is in
This magick is worked, with harm to none
So mote it be; there, it is done.

NUTMEG BUTTER RECIPE

This butter can be used as a lip balm, body oil, shampoo or face cream. Crush 6 nutmeg seeds using a mortar and pestle and add to a Mason jar. Pour ½ cup of carrier oil of your choice to the crushed nutmegs, ensuring they are covered. Seal the jar and sit it in direct sunlight for two to three days, shaking the jar twice a day. Strain the oil into a dark glass bottle and keep the butter in a dark, dry place.

15 Monday

16 Tuesday

17 Wednesday

Chelmsford Assizes, a periodic court for serious crime and witch trials in Essex, England.
Elizabeth Francis (1529-79) convicted three times for bewitchment and practising witchcraft;
she was executed after the third trial.

18 Thursday

19 Friday

Second hangings of the Salem witches in the United States; five women were executed in 1692.

20 Saturday

21 Sunday

Full moon.

22 Monday

Mother Agnes Waterhouse (1503–66), first woman executed in England for practising witchcraft.

23 Tuesday

24 Wednesday

25 Thursday

26 Friday

27 Saturday

Pendle witch trials started in 1612 in the York Assizes, a periodic court for serious crime and witch trials.

28 Sunday

Third quarter moon · Huntington Assizes, a periodic court for serious crime and witch trials; Mary Hicks, a witch of Huntington, and her nine-year-old daughter were both hanged for practising witchcraft in 1716.

WITCHY TIP

If you wish to colour, cut or grow your hair it is wise to work with the lunar phases of the moon, just as mermaids do. They understand how moon magick influences the ebb and flow of the tides of life, and how it also has a huge influence on the condition, length and growth of your hair.

NEW MOON MERMAID SPELL

Sit in front of a mirror at the magickal time of dusk during a new moon phase. Make a list of all your redeeming features and qualities, and love and appreciate them. Light a pink candle and say:

Mermaids surround me with magick of moon
Beauty abounds and will come about soon
I look in my mirror of magick and gaze
At the flame-lit glass, which reflects quite a haze
I focus upon the belle in my heart
And draw from its essence; a beautiful start
Image appears, I see with new eyes
Perception reveals an attractive surprise!

As you feel your internal beauty expand it will reflect back beautifully at you through the hearts and eyes of others, and of course through your magick mirror.

August

Corn, holly, grain moon

Celebration and gratitude of the grain harvest

This heady month of sun and fun is greeted as a time of opportunity and good fortune, for these are the carefree days of summer, when the dreams that were seeded at Imbolc come fully into fruition and are now ripe for the picking. The first hint of autumn is witnessed as the hottest part of summer makes its promise to wane, through its shortened days and the first grains ready to be harvested. It's time to reap the harvest of rewards and appreciate and bless everything that comes your way, as you make the most of the remaining light and warm weather before the fall and give thanks for the abundant growth of the passing season.

LUGHNASADH: 1 August

GODDESS: **Tailtiu (Celtic/Irish)**, goddess of
August and of the earth, the harvest and first grains;
the foster mother of the sun god Lugh.

MOTHER: maturity, gratitude for earthly, physical sustenance.

~ LUGHNASADH ~
Gratitude for the gifts of the earth

Lughnasadh, or Lammas, marks the very first harvest of the year and the gathering in of the grains. It is when the sun god Lugh is celebrated; he is cut down in his prime only to rise up again the following year. Our ancestors looked forward to this important and busy time of year: a time of plenty for feasting in celebration of the first harvest and for honouring the natural cycle of life, death and rebirth, represented as the spirit of John Barleycorn (also known as Jack in the Green and Robin Hood). His time will come again, but for now the seeds planted earlier in the year have grown into an abundant crop and are ready to be harvested and stored in the grain barns, to see out the cold and barren months to come.

LUGHNASADH INVOCATION

Today the wheel of the year doth stop
At Lammas, time to reap the crops
That were sown earlier this year
Celebrate the harvest cheer
Of wheat, of cereal, of the grain
Store it safely, before the wane
John Barleycorn is now cut down
From his prime, but look around
For Lugh, the sun god, shines from high
Over the fields from the sky
From Mother Earth we are blessed
Toil now over; soon can rest
But from the sow, what did you reap?
Is it good, or do you weep?
From hard work what have you earned?
Of the lesson, what is learned?
May the magic of this day
Bless you now in every way.

MOON MAGICK

Like a bolt out of the blue an unexpected event will occur, one that will turn your life upside down and make your witchy pointy shoes curl upwards in delight! You are the magick you have been waiting for, so you must have belief in the prodigy within. You are a wonder and have always stood out from the crowd. Expect a once-in-a-lifetime opportunity to knock very soon as you bathe in the bluish hue of this rare full moon. Setting your intentions at this auspicious time is super powerful and intensifies your abilities as an extraordinary occurrence seeks you out. Don't feel blue; instead, look at the wonder and miracles around you through magickal eyes, as chance meetings and offers come flooding in. Something rare and beautiful is found and a nonpareil item is uncovered.

BLUE MOON

No longer alone, under blue moon
Unusual events to come about soon
With dreams in my heart, occurrence to face
New wonder and miracles birthed to embrace
This moon magick is said and done
So mote it be, with harm to none.

BLUE MOON RITUAL

Fill a bottle with moon water, small blue crystals and deep blue dye and place the bottle under a blue moon. Write your intent on a piece of paper or in your grimoire with a feather pen and using the infused blue water. Once you have finished, wrap the piece of paper or your grimoire in blue satin or blue velvet cloth. Place a blue crystal on top such as lapis lazuli, azurite or tanzanite.

29 Monday
Jennet Preston hanged in 1612 at York Racecourse. Sarah Good hanged with four other women from the Salem witch trials in 1692.

30 Tuesday

31 Wednesday

1 Thursday
Lughnasadh.

2 Friday

3 Saturday

4 Sunday
New moon · Malin Matsdotter (1613–76), originally from Sweden and of Finnish descent, was burned as a witch.

5   Monday

6   Tuesday

7   Wednesday

8   Thursday

9   Friday
Akua Denteh (??) was beaten to death for practising witchcraft in Ghana in 2020.

10   Saturday
World Day against Witch Hunts was created after Akua Denteh was killed in Ghana.

11   Sunday

POPPET MAGICK

A poppet is a doll-like effigy usually made from coloured felt, wax or wood, but they can also be made from corn. At this time of year corn dollies are stuffed with materials from the grain harvest along with magickal items such as herbs, crystals, stones, sigils, names and prayers. Look after and treat the effigy carefully and with respect, for it is symbolic of the person it represents. This is called sympathetic magick, and it is as old as witchcraft itself. From healing, protection and prosperity to banishment and warding, poppets can be used to harm or heal. Stick a pin in the area needing healing or in the heart for love, or wrap the poppet with black string to bind it.

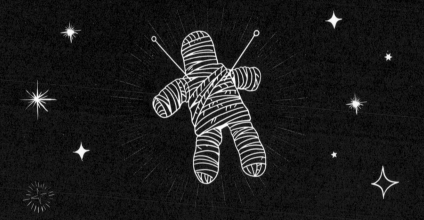

WITCHERY

This is what the various colours mean when used in a poppet:

BLACK
Binding and banishment

ORANGE
Success and happiness

BLUE
Healing

PURPLE
Protection

GREEN
Prosperity

RED
Love and passion

POPPET INCANTATION

Sticking pins, with witchy intent
Into doll-like fetish who doth represent
Those whom to banish, for love or to heal
Sorcery powers unveil and reveal
Poppet magick is worked with harm to none
So mote it be; there, it is done.

12 Monday

First quarter moon · Madame Helena Blavatsky (1831-91), Russian occultist, philosopher and co-founder of the Theosophical Society.

13 Tuesday

14 Wednesday

15 Thursday

16 Friday

17 Saturday

18 Sunday

Lancaster Assizes, a periodic court for serious crime and witch trials, held in 1612. Pendle and Samlesbury witches - nine women and one man - were found guilty of practising witchcraft.

AUGUST

19 Monday
Seasonal blue moon · Salem witch trials held in the United States in 1692; one woman and five men were hanged for practising witchcraft.

20 Tuesday
Pendle witches hanged in 1612 at Gallows Hill in Lancaster, United Kingdom.

21 Wednesday

22 Thursday

23 Friday

24 Saturday

25 Sunday
The entrance to Edinburgh Castle has a witches' well that commemorates the site where more than 300 women were burned at the stake. One of them was Dame Euphame MacCalzean, who was accused, among many other things, of using a spell to sink the ship of King James VI as it entered North Berwick.

PROSPERITY SPELL

Anoint a black candle with patchouli oil at the
third quarter moon on 26 August and say:

Money makes the world go round
Lack of it can make one frown
Shrug off, ignore, try to forget
Responsibility owns debt
Carve 'owned amount' on candle black
Anointing with oil, to pay it back
Flame determines what you earn
Debt's reduced as candle burns
Watch arrears melt away
Welcoming in a fat pay day.

Allow the candle to safely burn down
to completely banish debt.

26 Monday
Third quarter moon.

27 Tuesday

28 Wednesday

29 Thursday

30 Friday

31 Saturday
Raymond Buckland (1934–2017), high priest and occultist.

1 Sunday
First laws on spells and witchcraft passed in the Code of Hammurabi from 1754 BCE in ancient Mesopotamia.

SEPTEMBER

Harvest, hazel, fruit, barley moon

A time for gathering, resting, reflecting and celebration

As the cycle of the natural world moves further towards completion of the wheel of the year, we find ourselves on the cusp of transition just before the year begins to wane into darkness. Following the celebration of the grain harvest at Lughnasadh, which is now fully in and stored, the abundance and ripeness of the fruits of the earth the harvest queen bestows upon us at this time of year is acknowledged. The goddess is found in her mother aspect in the fading summer twilight or in the harvest moon.

As the full life of summer comes to an end we become witness to ripe fruits, nuts and squashes and the flaming autumn colours of red, orange and gold as nature turns in on herself, with the promise of the darker barren months of winter to come. This was a time of preparation, gathering and storing for our ancestors, as the final fruit and vegetable harvests were brought in and stored to last through the winter months. Traditionally workers were paid for the upcoming year, annual dues were collected and accounts were balanced. Nature's gifts are in abundance, and as the soft autumnal sun declines and autumnal mists descend, soft ripe fruit falls gently from the heavily laden trees that fill the glade. It is time to celebrate and draw from earth's bounty.

MABON: 21 September

GODDESS: Banbha (Celtic/Irish), earth mother, protection, fruitfulness, keeper of mystery.

MOTHER: contemplation, self-sufficiency, balance.

~ MABON ~

When day and night is in balance and the fruit harvest is celebrated.

Mabon is a recent name that has been adopted by witches and pagans alike to celebrate the autumn equinox, when daylight and darkness are in balance with each other and night and day are of equal length and in perfect equilibrium: dark and light, masculine and feminine, inner and outer. The name 'Mabon' is associated with Mabon, the Welsh god of mythology, and also with faery queen Mab, who rules over the Unseelie Court of autumn and winter.

At this time of balance and celebration we are reminded that we, too, are a part of nature. This is a time of going deep within, to rest after the labour of harvest, for reflection, to count your blessings for the abundance that has been bestowed upon you throughout the year. You must look at where you have been and what has been done during the preceding months and give thanks, which in turn will truly fill both your inner and outer gifts. This is when you reap what you had sown earlier in the year and harvest all that's now been made manifest from your earlier dreams and aspirations. It's a good time to let go of all that is no longer necessary and watch it fall away, just as the leaves do at this time of year.

As you acknowledge and embrace your shadow side, bring it into balance with the light that you already exude. Draw from the power of the cornucopia of abundance, a symbol for the wealth of harvest at Mabon, and balance your masculine and feminine energies so you can be both giving and receptive at this time of year in gratitude and perfect equilibrium.

MABON INCANTATION

Autumn's upon us, here at last
A time to reflect upon the past
Of the year that seems to have flown
Dreams were planted, now have grown
Mabon gifts us dark and light
Of perfect balance both day and night
And so we look deep down within
To check our equilibrium
Look back on past hurts, lessons learned
And use them so you won't get burned
Important to shine out far and wide
And to honour shadow side
For both together make you whole
The two as one complete your soul
Light two candles: one black, one white
Representing your joy and plight
Eliminate all you do not need
But keep what you have to succeed
The harvest's in, we give great cheer
And thanks for an abundant year.

2 Monday

3 Tuesday

New moon.

4 Wednesday

5 Thursday

6 Friday

7 Saturday

Margaret Ine Quaine (??) and John Cubbon (??) were executed in Castletown, Isle of Man in 1617. There is a memory plaque on Smelt Monument.

8 Sunday

9 Monday

10 Tuesday

Tiberius Claudius, Roman emperor from 41 to 54 CE, executed 45 men and 85 women for practising witchcraft.

11 Wednesday

First quarter moon · Silver RavenWolf (1956–), author of many books on witchcraft and wicca.

12 Thursday

13 Friday

14 Saturday

15 Sunday

MOON MAGICK

Fertility spells and rituals are ripe for the picking whenever the moon is invoked for some earth magick. Steeped in magick and mystery, this element forms the blood and bones of our physical bodies; from the earth we come and will one day return. Mother Earth nurtures and restores you, helping you to survive the physical, emotional and spiritual changes that accompany the rites of passage of conception through to your croning years. Acceptance turns the magickal key for smooth transformation to take place as she takes responsibility for those under her care, for she is the creator goddess of the land who ushers in new life at spring with all promises of fertility. She is also a destructor goddess whose cruel reign over winter leaves the land barren and fruitless, for in the cycle of life nature must die before it can rise up and grow again. For now, enjoy her bounty, as the land is abundant and her fruits of plenty are all waiting to be harvested.

Magick of moon, richness of earth
Bestow upon me your powers of birth
Strong grounding, growth, stability
New life restores fertility
This moon phasing magick is now said and done
So mote it be, with harm to none.

APPLE

I am the forbidden fruit – not because I am bad for you, but because I unveil that which is hidden. When you slice me in half my five seeds reveal a star, a pentagram, the exact same shape that Venus, the planet of love, forms when orbiting the earth. I invite you to bite through my ripe skin to taste my sweet flesh, for I am the fruit of the tree of life that holds the knowledge of all that humankind seeks. However, you would be wise to remember that some things are forbidden in order to keep you from harm.

WITCHY RECIPE:
NETTLE SOUP

This soup is great for gout and excess acid and as a blood purifier. Heat 1 tablespoon of olive oil in a large saucepan over a medium heat. Add vegetables of your choice such as carrots, celery, leeks, onions and potatoes and cook for 10 minutes. Add vegetable stock and cook for another 15 minutes or until soft. Add 300 grams of young nettle leaves and a few wild garlic leaves, then simmer for 2 minutes. Blend the mixture, return to the heat and add some milk, butter and seasoning to taste.

16 Monday

17 Tuesday
Partial lunar eclipse.

18 Wednesday
Full moon.

19 Thursday
Fulda witch trials held in Germany between 1603 and 1606. Merga Bien (1560-1603) burned alive.

20 Friday

21 Saturday
Mabon, autumn equinox.

22 Sunday
Salem witch trials in the United States between 1692 and 1693; eight people hanged for practising witchcraft.

23 Monday

24 Tuesday

Third quarter moon · North Berwick witch trials in the United Kingdom between 1590 and 1592; more than 70 people were executed.

25 Wednesday

26 Thursday

Witch-hunts are still being inflicted upon innocent women and men, from Sub-Saharan Africa, India, the Middle East, the Amazon and Papua New Guinea.

27 Friday

28 Saturday

29 Sunday

GODDESS MAGICK

Baba Yaga is honoured during the Slavic festivities of Obzinky, a pagan celebration of the harvest during the autumn equinox. The festival takes place on a Sunday after the harvest is brought in; the last sheaf of corn represents Baba Yaga and the decline of the growing seasons. As the expansion of darkness in the night sky envelops the earth, Baba Yaga steps into her power and claims the decaying season of autumn.

HARVEST GRATITUDE SPELL

Hold an apple and say:

Grateful for harvest, abundance of fruit
Scrumping for apples, grabbing my loot
Goddess as mother fades in twilight
Balance is key in rest or in fight
As I look to the year that's fleetingly past
I look at my wealth that's increasingly fast
My harvest is in, I'll reap my windfall
In honour and grace I give thanks for my all.

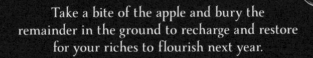

Take a bite of the apple and bury the remainder in the ground to recharge and restore for your riches to flourish next year.

OCTOBER

Blood, vine, hunter's moon

Season of witches and the olde Celtic year dies

October is the month we witness the death of nature. As leaves continue to fall we enjoy the vibrant colours of the season, darker nights and an abundance of squashes. Now that the harvest is in and celebrated at Mabon it's time to prepare fruit jam preserves and tinctures for colds and flu, using ingredients collected earlier from the earth, trees and hedgerows such as rose hips, apples and berries. The crone, who reigns over the harsher months, is cold and callous and beckons you with a bony finger to witness the death of nature and all that will assist you in moving forward.

SAMHAIN: 31 October

GODDESS: **Cerridwen (Celtic/Welsh)**, keeper of the gates between the worlds, grail goddess.

CRONE: bringer of darkness and death, of blood and bone; the underworld.

~ SAMHAIN ~

An honouring of the souls of the dead, when the veil between the worlds is at its thinnest.

Hallowe'en conjures up ghosts, pumpkin lanterns and children shouting 'Trick or Treat!' as they hungrily hold out bags for candy. It is celebrated at the end of October in both the northern and southern hemispheres. Traditionally called Samhain, this is an old Celtic celebration of summer's end. Fires were lit on the night of 31 October in the northern hemisphere and villagers would burn crops and animals to share with their gods and goddesses and to give thanks for the bounty of the harvest. The Celts believed that the souls of the dead of the underworld were set free for that night, some of which were welcomed and others feared. Costumes and masks were worn for protection from these spirits. The veil between the worlds at this time is at its thinnest, so we are more able to see and connect with the world of the fae and spirit.

Samhain is still considered to be a time of connection with and reflection on those who have left this world for the other, and to look at where we have journeyed from and to during the wheel of the year. The goddess in her triple form has become the crone, and we are invited to draw on her wisdom from deep within as she cradles us during the dark months to come, enabling us to release all that no longer serves us.

SAMHAIN INCANTATION

Cauldrons boiling, lanterns are shining
Ghouls and ghosts, groans and whining
Parties sweep across the land
Children, adults, hand in hand
Time of fun but must remember
As fires burn bright and glow with embers
Our ancestors who walked before
We honour thee and ask for more
Wisdom, tools, to help us be
The wise among us, let us see
Through veil, while thin, this very night
Protection in place, no need for fright
We welcome you and all you bring
Go deep inside and look within
To shed the old, a shamanic death
Embraced and warmed within the earth
Inviting in life anew
The goddess calls for it to be you
Through the year from maiden to mother
The end is now, to feel the other
In her glory stands the crone
Don't be afraid to stand alone
This sacred path leads you to be free
Go forth in strength. So mote it be.

30 Monday

1 Tuesday

It is estimated that more than 200,000 witches were burned or hanged in Western Europe.

2 Wednesday

New moon, annular solar eclipse · Arthur Edward Waite (1857-1942), occultist, magician, alchemist and co-creator of the Rider-Waite tarot.

3 Thursday

4 Friday

5 Saturday

6 Sunday

7 Monday

8 Tuesday

9 Wednesday

Flavia Kate Peters (1968-), high priestess, faery seer and occultist, United Kingdom.

10 Thursday

First quarter moon.

11 Friday

12 Saturday

Aleister Crowley (1875-1947), English occultist, high priest and ceremonial magician.

13 Sunday

All Templars living in France in 1307 were arrested and condemned for heresy and practising witchcraft. This is one supposed origin of Friday the 13th being unlucky.

WITCH'S WISDOM

The pull of darkness is all consuming when the crone is exposed, and you should be careful not to be drawn into the shadows for this is when the darkness seems most inviting. The crone is the mistress of magick, and light can only be seen through the darkness. Both have a necessary purpose and cannot exist without the other, so allow the crone to envelop her dark cloak around you to block out the comfort zone you've been holding on to so tightly. It is the only way for you to truly see.

As you take up your sword and battle through the dark forest you will be blind for a while, with only the crone as unwelcome company to guide you. She will take you to the darkest place to shed light on that which you are seeking. She will teach you how to draw strength from the dark mystery and claim the force and power that reside in the depths of your soul. Everything is in place to support the cycle of life and death, to bring about the magickal transformation you desire. As the midwife of your rebirth she changes everything she touches.

WITCHERY

The crone is a symbol of death, destruction and decay.

She is the grandmother, the divine hag aspect of the triple goddess. She is the most feared and most often avoided, and is portrayed as the evil witch in faery tales. The crone has a fearful shadow side, for it is darkness that accompanies her through the winter months and ultimately to death. However, death is not the end for witches, who await the crone's gift of magickal transformation and promise of rebirth.

CRONE

ASPECTS: wisdom, repose, magick, destruction, decay, death.

SEASON: winter.

COLOUR: black.

MOON PHASES: waning, dark, new.

FESTIVALS: Samhain, Yule.

14 Monday

Patrica Crowther (1927-), early mother of modern Wicca and high priestess, United Kingdom.

15 Tuesday

16 Wednesday

17 Thursday

Super full moon, almost total lunar eclipse.

18 Friday

19 Saturday

20 Sunday

Selena Fox (1949-), Wiccan priestess and pagan elder.

21 Monday

22 Tuesday

Witch trials were held in Torsåker, Sweden in 1674–75; 71 people were beheaded and burned as witches.

23 Wednesday

Julie Aspinall (1964–), high priestess of the Coven of Gaia.

24 Thursday

Third quarter moon · More than 2,000 magickal books were burned by Emperor Augustus of Rome in 31 BCE.

25 Friday

26 Saturday

27 Sunday

CERRIDWEN'S MESSAGE

Stirring the cauldron of emotional darkness was your invitation to me. It is a dangerous path of the mind you have been treading and it led you to become shrouded by other people's negative comments, blames and projections. Your perception is healing now from a warped and negative outlook and is in need of some magickal transformation. Allow me, the keeper of the cauldron, to brew up a magickal potion especially for you. Drink of the wisdom and knowledge I offer you and allow the scales to fall from your eyes to see the beauty that awaits you. Allow me to plant the seeds of change within your sacred womb, which I promise will birth transformation and the power of your own feminine divinity.

---○---

CAULDRON INCANTATION

Hubble, bubble, cast out trouble
Clear your mind now on the double
Sip of magick from her potions
Ideas inspire creative notions.

HONOURING THE ANCESTORS

Ancestors of blood and bone
Of those remembered and unknown
Ancient past found in reflection
Honouring a deep connection
Forgotten, past and ancient too
We give up thanks to honour you
Rest in peace but guide us well
Secrets deep but ne'er to tell
Ancestors of blood and bone
From earth you have to spirit flown
Ancestral lines now heal at last
We break free from the chains of past
To all those who've gone before
We've gone full circle, becoming more
All honour, prayers for what you've done
Let's celebrate all that I've won
You are the ancestors, who walked this land
I'll rewrite history and boldly stand
Old wounds healed, now we're free
I am the ancestors, and you are me.
Ancestry magick worked with harm to none.
So mote it be; there, it is done.

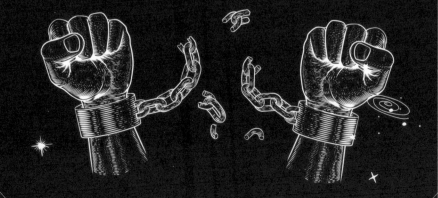

28 Monday

29 Tuesday

30 Wednesday

31 Thursday

Samhain, Hallowe'en. A time to honour the ancestors who have gone before us in the name of witchcraft who have been persecuted, burned, drowned, hanged and stoned.

1 Friday

Full moon · More than 170 women were executed in Rome in 331 BCE for practising witchcraft.

2 Saturday

3 Sunday

Petronilla de Meath (1300–24) was burned at the stake in Kilkenny, Ireland. This was the first known case in Ireland and the United Kingdom of death by fire for heresy.

KITCHEN WISDOM

ELDERFLOWER: steeped in mystery and superstition, my ancient history is shared among British hedgerows. Protected by the elder mother, who resides in the trunk of my tree, I will ward off evil spirits and protect your home from misfortune if I'm planted near the threshold. The powerful warding property of my leaves will assist in breaking spells cast against you and will undo any harmful intentions. Allow me to deflect any ill will as I defend and guard your magickal honour. As you sleep deeply beneath the canopy of my white, lacy, fragrant flowers you are invited into a parallel existence, into the mystical dimension of the faeries, who are fundamental to the magick of your spell work. The nature spirits will ward off any negative or victim beliefs that are blocking you as you harness your natural magickal abilities.

ELDERFLOWER: WARDING

Defend, protect, I'll guard you well
And ward off any misused spell
Faery secrets hidden deep
Ancient magic's yours to keep
This magic is worked, with harm to none.
So mote it be; there, it is done.

WITCHY RECIPE

This cordial is great for sweating and as a diuretic and for treating the effects of the flu and sinusitis. Put 500 grams of caster sugar and 4 tablespoons of honey into a large saucepan with 1 litre of spring or filtered water. Bring to the boil then immediately remove from the heat. Add the peeled rind from two unwaxed lemons and 18 elderflower heads to the pan, making sure they are covered by the liquid. Add the juice of the lemons, put the lid on and allow the mixture to infuse for one day. Strain the cordial and pour it into bottles or jars. Store in a dark place.

PENTAGRAM PROTECTION

The pentagram is a sign of good and of the goddess. It holds supernatural powers of protection and connects you to the potent forces of nature when it comes to working magickally. Use it for protection in your magickal practice as well as day to day to spiritually shield yourself against malevolence and negative elements and to connect with the forces of nature. Each of the five points symbolises each of the basic elements: earth, air, fire, water and spirit. You can only grow stronger with the pentagram at your side. It is time to make a stand and proudly show the world who you are, with reverence, as you cast aside all fears of the past and shine out brightly like the star you are.

PENTAGRAM INCANTATION

Star of witches, five points of power
Fetish in place with strength to empower
Stand firm in convictions, of honour, respect
Symbol of ancients to restore and protect
Pentagram magick is worked with harm to none
So mote it be; there, it is done.

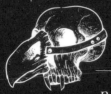

NOVEMBER

Snow, ivy, dark moon

Reassessment, embracing loss, acceptance

Happy New Year! After the death of the year that was witnessed at Samhain, 1 November is celebrated by witches as All Hallow's Day, the start of the new Celtic year and the beginning of winter. However, November is regarded as being an autumnal month that offers a mix of cold and bright, as burned-orange leaves continue to fall in the chill. The weather can be confusing with its bright sunshine accompanying much colder days, which brings with it the promise of hard frost and sometimes snow. These harsh, biting days are a good time to defend yourself and define your boundaries with others and for darker magick to ward off harm.

As you prepare to face the harshness of winter yet to come you can also rejoice in a month of festivities, of thanksgiving, fireworks and remembrance. It's a time of rain and great storms and therefore a good time for weather witching!

GODDESS: **The Morrighan (Irish/Celtic)**, battle goddess
of death and war, bane magick, the darker arts.

CRONE: death and rebirth, sovereignty, inner strength.

WEATHER MAGICK

As a weather witch you should be able to determine which way the winds blow as the light of the silvery moon streams clarity through your mind, enhancing your intellect and illuminating your inner world. Focus on the sacred space within during this month of reflection to nourish your creative spirit and expand your imagination. When the element of air blows through the power of your mind, all visions, dreams and insights are richly enhanced and you are urged to believe that what you see within is indeed real. Imagination is the secret portal to the otherworld, the gateway to magick. Vivid colours or pictures when you close your eyes, repetitive signs and symbols are confirmed as coded messages.

All possibilities are carried upon the four winds that breathe forth your thoughts and dreams into this reality and dimension. All you need do is trust what you see within and believe.

WEATHER INCANTATION

Storms blow in with all their might
Illuminating sacred sight
Visions, dreams, trust to see
Imagination is the key
Weather magick is said and done
So mote it be, with harm to none.

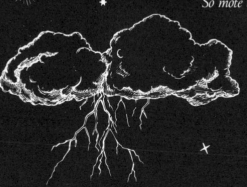

MOON MAGICK

Your secret wish to summon up authoritative power, to whip up a storm with the click of your fingers and work your magick with effective control presents powers of possibilities in the highest form. Feelings of inadequacy or low self-esteem would be a thing of the past if only you could manage that invisible source called energy effectively, like all powerful witches. Release the fears that prevent you from reclaiming your inner power and step into your full sovereignty. As the full moon hangs in the sky on 15 November, embrace its power as you draw down its magick, mystery and the embodiment of the goddess., for she is the vessel from which all things spring forth. Feel the power of the goddess surging through you and allow her to move and work through you as you accept her gift of empowerment. Soon you will have control over your life and the confidence to support others while standing in your power.

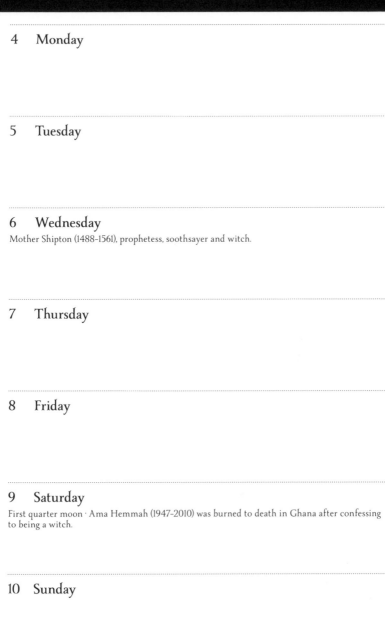

4   Monday

5   Tuesday

6   Wednesday
Mother Shipton (1488-1561), prophetess, soothsayer and witch.

7   Thursday

8   Friday

9   Saturday
First quarter moon · Ama Hemmah (1947-2010) was burned to death in Ghana after confessing to being a witch.

10   Sunday

11 Monday

The witch of Endor was the first witch written about in the Old Testament (1 Samuel 28:3-25).
She was a female sorcerer who was visited by Saul, the first king of Israel as she owned a
talisman that could summon the dead. She predicted Saul's downfall.

12 Tuesday

13 Wednesday

14 Thursday

15 Friday

Full moon.

16 Saturday

17 Sunday

GODDESS RITUAL

This invocation embodies the goddess, symbolised by the moon. The high priestess enters into trance and draws the goddess inside her, who speaks through her. Wear a special robe that makes you feel powerful and sprinkle a circle of salt around you. Stand with your arms outstretched to the moon and your feet apart.

Say this incantation:

On this bright night I draw down the moon
Oh goddess, speak through me, empower me soon
Fears to face first, a journey within
Power reclaimed, let the ritual begin
This moon magick is now done
So mote it be, with harm to none.

KITCHEN WISDOM

WITCH HAZEL: a sensitive witch is often a troubled witch, at least emotionally. When you wear your heart on your sleeve you become an open book of shadows, and that can land you in sticky situations. As you focus more on your magickal work you will find that your intuition heightens, as does your sensitivity. Avoiding those who make you sore along with those who would rather see you with a blemished reputation does not serve a fragile soul such as yourself. Rich in tannins, my natural plant compound's powerful antioxidant properties cast soothing, healing spells on most dermatology issues and banish the dark circles under your eyes, as well as troublesome emotions and negativity when used in a herbal elixir. Instead of becoming thick skinned, allow me as nature's astringent to relieve you of any irritation or pains in the backside as you learn to appreciate and hone your empathetic nature.

WITCH HAZEL: SENSITIVITY

I'm one witch who's invited in
I'll banish zits and soothe your skin
Divining twigs draw up emotion
Heart now healed with magic potion.

WITCHY RECIPE

This toner is excellent for clearing a face of acne and to tighten pores and maintain the skin's natural PH balance.
Add the following to a Mason jar: 1 cup of witch hazel extract, ½ cup of apple cider vinegar, ½ cup of distilled water, 10 drops of tea tree oil, 1 teaspoon of vitamin E oil and 2 teaspoons of aloe vera gel. Stir to combine. You can use different oils such as rose oil; everyone's skin is different, so personalise the toner to suit you.

18   Monday

19   Tuesday

20   Wednesday

21   Thursday

22   Friday

Franz Hartmann (1838-1912), occultist, doctor, astrologer and theosophist.

23   Saturday

Third quarter moon.

24   Sunday

25 Monday
Helen Duncan (1897-1956) was the last person imprisoned under the Witchcraft Act of 1735.

26 Tuesday

27 Wednesday

28 Thursday

29 Friday

30 Saturday
Ralph Harvey (1928-2020), occultist, high priest and teacher.

1 Sunday
New moon · Malleus Maleficarum (Hammer of Witches), written in 1486 by a Catholic clergymen, was published in 1487 and endorsed the extermination of witches. This book had a strong influence on witch trials that followed.

DARK CRONE RITUAL

Place a black cloth on the ground and a black candle to the right and a white candle to the left. In between both candles, place some bones. Set an offering of bread and red wine in front of the bones and light the candles.

Gaze into the flames, then stretch your
arms out to the crone and say:

Oh, divine hag, goddess of death
Hidden in view 'til my last dying breath
As I face the dark, embraced in the light
I seek thy hallows, for all's not black and white
Goddess of crone, woman of bone
For all my misgivings I wish to atone
A keeper of secrets, I'll not deny
Bless me as I seek you, for I'm ready to die
Grant me your blessings, I wish to transform
As I stand in ritual, arms stretched to perform
I invoke you now, to connect as one
So mote it be, with harm to none.

Let the candles safely burn down and
pour the wine onto the ground for the
crone to receive in the underworld.

DECEMBER

Wolf, elder, cold moon

◇

A time of quiet introspection and expectation

Winter is a mystical artist that paints a breathless picture of landscapes adorned in jewels of sparkling frost and glistening ice. It's a time when your breath is visible on a cold, brisk day, when trees stand stark and bare and nature is stripped of its former glory to its very core.

This is a season when mystery hangs in the air as dark nights draw in, enveloping the weakened, low-slung sun, and when the earth is steeped in deep magick and mystery that nurtures and restores all that resides within it. It is a time of looking deep within and withdrawing into your inner cave.

December is a month of hardship and discomfort that ensures trials and tribulations for those ancestors who faced the glacial callousness of winter, for she is a harsh taskmaster who takes no prisoners. It is a time for change, when you acknowledge and honour the cycles of death and rebirth. It's a time when hope is renewed and, like the trees of the season, you are stripped bare, naked and vulnerable as the macabre presence of the crone shrouds you.

◇

YULE: 21 December

◇

GODDESS: Cailleach (Celtic/Scottish), the crone who rules over winter begins to fade as the returning sun shines new promises of hope, light and a fresh dawn.

CRONE: hideous queen of winter, bearer of storms, instigator of death.

~ YULE ~

A celebration of the rebirth of the sun, from the darkness growing into the light

Yule is the sabbat of the winter solstice, the shortest day and the least productive time in nature's annual cycle. This is the longest night, more than 12 hours of darkness as we wait for the dawn. The tradition of a mid-winter festival is ancient and was one our ancestors looked forward to through the cold barren days of December.

Yule is a celebration of the rebirth of the sun, for after the longest night the sun will again begin to grow stronger. It is a sacred time of solar rebirth when we bring into our homes the Yule log for the returning sun, mistletoe for fertility and holly for protection. This sabbat represents the rebirth of light. Here, on the longest night of the year, the goddess gives birth to the sun god and hope for new light is reborn.

This is a time-honoured tradition when our ancestors and faeries alike would gather to welcome the return of the sun. At winter solstice the sun appears at its weakest, having waned in strength since peaking at the summer solstice, or Litha, six months earlier. Great cheers ring out in celebration, for on the very next winter's morn the sun starts its ascent as it heads towards the summer months once again. The birth of the sun; the light of the world; the new king is heralded!

This time the oak king prevails over the holly king to bring us the light half of the year. The holly king is the overseer of holly trees; he rules the forests and woods during autumn and winter after battling with the oak king at the summer solstice. They battle again at Yule when the oak king, guardian of oak trees, wins and rules the forests and woods over the spring and summer. Their battle reflects the balance of the seasons: the wheel has turned and we celebrate the re-emergence of light out of darkness, bringing renewal of life and the promise of a successful future.

YULE INCANTATION

Faery folk tiptoe soft
Across the land of snow and frost
Towards a holly tree at Yule
'tis time to cut it from its rule
For in this battle, oak king wins
To lord over months to take through spring
And in the morn turn to the sun
Who is born again, the light has won!
Each year the sacred wheel doth turn
Now Yuletide's here, 'tis our concern
To celebrate with joy and mirth
May bells ring out for peace on earth
So place the logs upon the fire
And make wishes of heart's desire
Honour the flames that warm the cool
With blessings to one and all this Yule.

2 Monday

Franz Bardon the magician (1909-58), magician, occultist and teacher of Hermetics.

3 Tuesday

More than 123 people were persecuted in India for practising sorcery and witchcraft between 2016 and 2019.

4 Wednesday

5 Thursday

Pope Innocent VIII published a papal bull in 1484 that condemned witchcraft.

6 Friday

Dion Fortune (1890-1946), occultist and ceremonial magician.

7 Saturday

8 Sunday

First quarter moon.

9   Monday

10   Tuesday

11   Wednesday

12   Thursday

Amina Bint Abdul Halim bin Salem Nasser (??) beheaded in Saudi Arabia in 2011 for practising witchcraft.

13   Friday

14   Saturday

15   Sunday

Full moon · Anna Franklin (1955-), high priestess and bestselling author of more than 20 books on witchcraft.

CRONE WISDOM

I am the one you fear, for I am the bringer of death. I am everything you have been avoiding, yet it is I who is the answer to your wishes and dreams and the future you hope for. It is I who holds the keys to transformation in the highest.

For every stumbling block you face I shall be waiting at the top of the highest mountain for you to reach the summit. I know you have the power within and all the tools you need to step into the light. Now is the time to allow the emptiness, the barren void within, to start germinating, and for that to occur the process of death must begin. Allow old beliefs and behaviours that do not serve the new you to dissolve. Let the old energy seep back down into the earth to transmute and transform into the hardness of the rocks and cruel terrain of the wilds. You have nothing to fear, for I will watch over you. You will find me in the rugged hills, the icy glaciers, each stone and the snowy mountains. I am the bone mother, the keeper of winter, the bringer of death.

CRONE INCANTATION

Born to survive, fight for life
Sufferance of tears and strife
Darkness shadows over light
Claiming death through blackened night.

HERNE THE HUNTER

December and the winter solstice are Herne the Hunter's time.
He exists in the woods and is another face of the green man.
Many attune to him during their solstice celebrations and throughout
the month, and animals that are associated with snowy climes and
antlered beasts are sacred to him. Herne is lord of the Greenwood,
bringing the depths of winter in his wake. Statues of stags and reindeer
are often placed on altars and other locations at this time of year to
honour him and this time of year.

DECEMBER

16 Monday
In Tanzania more than 40,000 people have been accused of practising witchcraft; many were tried and killed between 1960 and 2000.

17 Tuesday

18 Wednesday
Edith Rose Woodford-Grimes (1887–1975), one of the first adherents of English Wicca and the working partner of Gerald Gardner.

19 Thursday
Ronald Hutton (1953–), historian specialising in witchcraft, paganism and British folklore.

20 Friday

21 Saturday
Yule, winter solstice, midwinter.

22 Sunday
Third quarter moon.

23 Monday

24 Tuesday

25 Wednesday

26 Thursday

27 Friday

28 Saturday

29 Sunday

STAG'S MESSAGE

I have chosen to cross your path at this time to assist you in your quest to hunt down and know your own spiritual strengths and insights. You have been given a great gift of second sight, passed down through your ancestral line, and it is time to reawaken those gifts of intuition and sensitivity. It is time to stand tall and be seen, for you've hidden the premonitions you've witnessed. With age comes wisdom. Your majestic spirit, along with mine, will fuse together as we walk between the worlds of magick and the mundane.

When you acknowledge your supernatural abilities you will be more able to rise above any challenges that are presented. Stag magick will determine whether the feelings, signs and visions you're getting are foreboding or favourable, and trusting your instincts is a sure-footed way of mastering that feeling or hunch that should not be ignored.

STAG: PREMONITION

Sneaky feeling, sixth sense feared
Spooky sightings, being weird
Trust in a forest king's suspicion
Be warned and heed the premonition.

WITCHY TIP

Use stag antlers when working with fire magick to move coal and rocks. Wear stag antlers on your head to empower visions. Make an antler necklace for strength and protection. Stag is associated with the horned god in his many incarnations. Both Artemis and Diana, goddesses of the hunt, are guardians of the forest with the stag as a symbol.

HERB WREATH

Use sprigs of rosemary, sage, thyme, basil and mint to make a special wreath that will invite goodwill and cheer to your table. Decorate the setting with cloves, cranberries and a sprinkling of ginger. You may even wish to select ingredients from the wreath itself as you prepare your seasonal feast.

As you make your wreath and
prepare your feast say:

I'll make a wreath and carefully weave
Fine ingredients to achieve
A tasty treat for you and me
A Yuletide feast of satiety
From this wreath I'll carefully choose
A herb or two I'd like to use
Its magick gives the food a lift
With thanks let's consume winter's gift
Yule magick is weaved with harm to none
The light has burst forth. There, it is done.

Hang the wreath on your front door
to welcome in the nature spirits from
the cold, in true Yule tradition.

30 Monday

Black moon (the second new moon of the month): a sacred time for harnessing extra power for banishment spells and working with the shadow side · Maxine Sanders (1946–), high priestess and occultist.

31 Tuesday

1 Wednesday

2 Thursday

3 Friday

4 Saturday

5 Sunday

WITCHES OF ROYALTY 2024

ANNE BOLEYN, *Queen of England*
Born: 1501 or 1507. Died: 1536
Briefly accused of using witchcraft against her husband Henry VIII,
which led to her death by beheading on 19 May

JOAN OF NAVARRE, *Queen of England*
Born: 1368. Died: 10 June 1437
Accused of witchcraft

ELEANOR COBHAM, *Duchess of Gloucester*
Born: c.1400. Died: 7 July 1452
Accused of practising witchcraft and died in prison

JACQUETTA WOODVILLE, *Duchess of Bedford*
Born: c.1416. Died: 30 May 1472
Accused of practising witchcraft

ELIZABETH WOODVILLE, *Queen of England*
Born: c.1437. Died: 8 June 1492
Accused of practising witchcraft

JANET DOUGLAS, *Lady Glamis*
Born: c.1498. Died: 17 July 1537
Accused of practising witchcraft and burned at the stake

CATHERINE DE' MEDICI, *Queen of France*
Born: 13 April 1519. Died: 5 January 1589
Accused of practising witchcraft

ISABELLA OF ANGOULÊME, *queen consort to King John*
Born: c.1186. Died: 4 June 1246
Accused of practising witchcraft

GUNNHILD, *Viking queen*
Born: c.910. Died: 980 CE
Thrown alive into a bag and drowned
for practising witchcraft.

WITCHES' MUSEUMS, MEMORIALS AND PLACES TO VISIT

Arnemetia's Mystical Emporium, Buxton, UK
Mother Shipton's Cave, Knarebrough, UK
Museum of Witchcraft and Magic, Boscastle, Cornwall, UK
Pendle Heritage Centre, Barrowford, Lancaster, UK
Museum of Witchcraft and Wizardry, Stratford on Avon, UK
Salem Witch Museum and Memorial, Salem, Massachusetts, USA
Buckland Museum of Witchcraft and Magic, Cleveland, Ohio, USA
New Orleans Historic Voodoo Museum, New Orleans, Louisiana, USA
Museum of Icelandic Sorcery and Witchcraft, Hólmavík, Iceland.
Witches Weigh House, Oudewater, Netherlands
Magicum – Berlin Magic Museum, Berlin, Germany
Hexenmuseum Schweiz, Gränichen, Switzerland
Witches Museum, Zugarramurdi, Spain
West Cornwall Museum of Magic and Folklore, Falmouth, UK
Museum of Witchcraft, São Paulo, Brazil

WITCH ORGANISATIONS

Children of Artemis
Witchcraft.org

UK Pagan Federation
Paganfed.org

NOTES

Witchy fact

In 1944 Jane Rebecca Yorke (1872-1953), an English medium, was the last person tried and convicted under the Witchcraft Act 1735 for her claims she could talk to the dead who had died in World War 2. She was found guilty on seven counts, but instead of being burned alive she was sentenced to good behaviour for three years and fined £5 at an East London Court. The Witchcraft Act was phased out in the 1950s.

NOTES

Witchy fact

Suspected witches would travel long distances to Oudewater in the Netherlands to purchase official certificates stating that they were heavier than air according to the town's scales. These certificates stated that they were unable to fly and were less likely to be considered witches, therefore ensuring that the test of a witch by drowning was not applied to said witch.

NOTES

NOTES

NOTES